THE GREATEST GIFT

THE
GREATEST
GIFT

*The Courageous Life and Death
of Sister Dorothy Stang*

BINKA LE BRETON

DOUBLEDAY
New York London Toronto Sydney Auckland

PUBLISHED BY DOUBLEDAY

Copyright © 2007 by Binka Le Breton

All Rights Reserved

Published in the United States by Doubleday, an imprint of
The Doubleday Broadway Publishing Group, a division of
Random House, Inc., New York
www.doubleday.com

DOUBLEDAY and the portrayal of an anchor with a dolphin
are registered trademarks of Random House, Inc.

Photos © 2008 by the Sisters of Notre Dame de Namur
and the Stang Family.
Photographs appear courtesy
of the Sisters of Notre Dame de Namur
and the Stang Family.

Book design by Jennifer Ann Daddio

Library of Congress Cataloging-in-Publication Data
Le Breton, Binka.
The greatest gift : the courageous life and death of Sister
Dorothy Stang / Binka Le Breton.
p. cm.
Includes bibliographical references and index.
1. Stang, Dorothy (Dorothy Mae), d. 2005. 2. Sisters of
Notre Dame de Namur—United States—Biography.
3. Sisters of Notre Dame de Namur—Brazil—Biography. I. Title.
BX4705.S7938L4 2007
271'.97—dc22
[B]   2007023379

ISBN 978-0-385-52218-2

PRINTED IN THE UNITED STATES OF AMERICA

1   3   5   7   9   10   8   6   4   2

First Edition

To the Sisters of Notre Dame de Namur

CONTENTS

CONTENTS

LIST OF
PHOTOGRAPHS

BRAZILIAN AMAZÔNIA
South America

Venezuela

Guyana   French Guiana

Colombia   Suriname

                Roraima

Ecuador   Amapá

        Amazon River

Peru   Amazonas   Pará   Maranhão   Ceará   Rio Grande do Norte

    Acre   Piauí   Paraíba

                                                            Pernambuco

        Rondônia   Tocantins   Alagoas

            Mato Grosso   Bahia   Sergipe

                        Brasília

Bolivia   Goiás

                            Minas Gerais

            Mato Grosso   Espírito Santo
            do Sul   São Paulo

Chile   Paraguay   Rio de Janeiro

                    Paraná

                        Santa Catarina

            Rio Grande
            do Sul

        Uruguay

    Argentina

        ⧄ Amazônia   Brazil

0 250 500   1,000
Kilometers

N

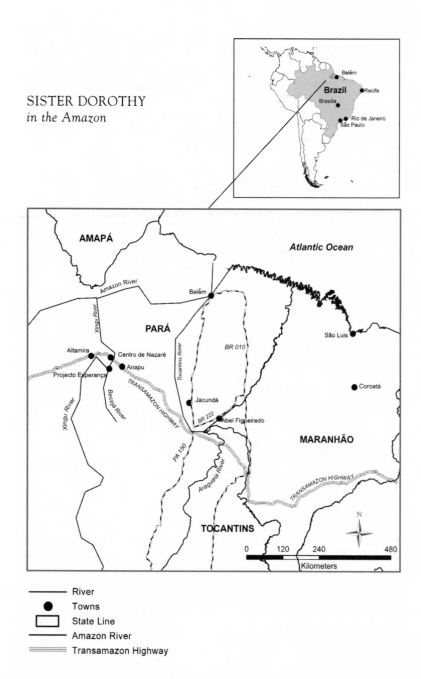

SISTER DOROTHY
in the Amazon

Belém

Brazil
Recife
Brasília
Rio de Janeiro
São Paulo

AMAPÁ

Atlantic Ocean

Amazon River

Belém

PARÁ

São Luís

Altamira
Centro de Nazaré
BR 010
Anapu
Projecto Esperança

Coroatá

Xingu River
Bacajá River

TRANSAMAZON HIGHWAY

Tocantins River

Xingu River

Jacundá

BR 222
Abel Figueiredo

MARANHÃO

PA 150

Araguaia River

TRANSAMAZON HIGHWAY

TOCANTINS

N

0   120   240   480

Kilometers

River
Towns
State Line
Amazon River
Transamazon Highway

FOREWORD

Sister Dorothy Stang was murdered in the Amazon forest of Brazil. However, she is not to be considered a victim of murder. Victims of murder have no choice; their lives are taken. No one took the life of Sister Dorothy Stang. She had a choice. Dorothy gave her life freely and totally. She gave her life all of her life. That is what is unique about this missionary nun.

I remember standing with Dorothy in the parking lot of our provincial house the summer before she died. Knowing what the answer would be, I asked, "Dot, are you sure that you want to go back to Brazil?" We all knew that there was a price on her head. She looked at me incredulously and replied, "These are my people. I want to go back to be with them in their struggle." How could I have thought otherwise?

Dot found the meaning of life in self-giving love. As a middle child in her family of nine brothers and sisters, she quickly learned the give-and-take of family life. She seemed to place herself in the giving stance quite often. She became a Sister of Notre Dame de Namur so that she could give herself on behalf of people who are poor and uneducated. This passionate desire was not rooted in a martyr complex. Dorothy found great joy in her gift of self. She loved the people she worked with—the children in Chicago and Phoenix classrooms, the Mexican migrant families, the Brazilian peasant farmers. There was laughter and fun wherever she went and whomever she worked with.

That simple focus on the good of others is the message that continues to inspire all who know of her life and mission. Dorothy Stang cared about people and she cared about this good Earth, which is home to us all. She never thought about what she was giving up by living and working in the Amazon jungle. She did not concentrate on the danger of standing with the powerless. She simply and joyfully gave all she had. She met the forces of greed and destruction with hope for a better future. I believe that Dorothy faced her killers with the same peace and hope that characterized her entire life. This is her gift to all who knew her or who have heard her story. Her person is affirmation that there is meaning in life; there is hope; a self-giving life continues even after the last breath is taken.

If this simple, fun-loving, courageous person could spend a lifetime reverencing the dignity of every person, then maybe we can do the same. Dorothy Stang's love of people can inspire in us a sense of human kinship as we experience a kind of global interconnectedness unknown to previous generations. Because Dorothy embraced and cared for this wonderful Planet Earth, we are encouraged to do the same. Her joy in giving up the "good life" speaks to us, the 18 percent of the world's population who use 80 percent of the world's resources. Her life tells us that we too can free ourselves from the slavery of consumerism and live more simply so that others can simply live. Dorothy Stang, a little lady from Ohio, has a big message for our world.

—Sister Elizabeth Bowyer SND de N
Sisters of Notre Dame de Namur

INTRODUCTION

Tsunamis and terrorist attacks, car bombs and carnage, hurricanes and holocaust, huge disasters and tiny private griefs—all alter the smooth course of our lives and bring us unwillingly face-to-face with the fragility of our existence. How, then, shall we live our one life so that it makes a difference?

The problems are so large and we are so insignificant. Yet across the world thousands of nameless people daily choose to undertake acts of courage, large and small, with consequences that reach out through time and space to inspire and encourage the rest of us. One of them was a woman named Dorothy. She died on a red dirt road in the Amazon jungle because she believed passionately that people should care for the land and that in return the land would supply them with what they need, and she devoted her life to helping bring that dream to reality.

Amid a cast of national and international actors and ranging from the marble offices of the presidential palace in Brasília to the tiniest settlements in the farthest reaches of the forest, 20 million Brazilians are struggling against the heat, the mud, and the mosquitoes to make a living. Or a killing. From uncontacted indigenous tribes in the depths of the jungle to workers in the huge industrial complex at Carajás, from scientists in their laboratories to soldiers patrolling the frontiers, from subsistence farms to gigantic soybean projects, from clandestine cocaine processing plants to paved roads cutting ever deeper into the heart of the forest, men and women labor to preserve the pristine forest or to destroy it, to save souls or to enslave bodies, to assemble electronic goods, to dredge the rivers for gold dust, to pay their bills, and to feed their families.

The sheer scale of the Amazon blows your mind. One-fifth of all the fresh water on Earth. Thirty percent of all the biodiversity on the planet. Billions of dollars' worth of minerals in the red soil. Land without end.

Dorothy knew about the myths of land without end. She came from Ohio, where the gentle, rolling hills of the American East give way to the endless rolling prairies, once covered so thickly with bison that it seemed they too would never end. Dorothy understood the need to care for the land and to care for people's bodies and souls. Her religious vocation led her to join the Sisters of Notre Dame de Namur, women with hearts as wide as the world, and took her to the little town of Anapu on the Transamazon Highway in Brazil. There she worked with the poorest of the poor, learning with them the delicate balance of farming the forest soils without destroying the forest.

Dorothy was greatly loved and fiercely hated. The area where she worked was a rich land, well watered, close to the highway. Stands of valuable timber attracted the attention of local landowners dreaming of green pastures stocked with floppy-eared white cattle or fields of soybeans. They considered such land too good to be used for subsistence farming by peasants and sought to force the peasants out through intimidation: burning houses, scattering quick-growing grass seeds to choke the crops, sending gunmen to reinforce their message. And yet their path was blocked by a seventy-three-year-old foreign woman who had the nerve to tell the gunmen that they were wrong.

Dorothy refused to be silenced. When she saw injustice, she spoke out for the victims. She organized a straggling band of peasants into a community, she found money for them to set up small projects processing the fruits they grew on their plots, and she gave them a new confidence that they could take charge of their lives and not be forever victimized.

In such a small community everyone knows who is who, so Dorothy knew her enemies and reported their names to the federal police, demanding protection for the farmers. It never came. And on February 12, 2005, Dorothy was ambushed on a red dirt road in the forest and died, another victim of the senseless violence in the Amazon.

But her story doesn't end there.

The news was carried across the airwaves and through cyberspace to the whole world. Her story attracted attention because she was a woman, a nun, and a foreigner. Among the hundreds of forgotten killings that took place before her death and all the deaths to come, Dorothy's story crystallizes for us the certainty that one person, one deed, one act of courage, can make a difference.

I never met Dorothy, although we spoke a couple of times on a crackling telephone line. I had been researching and writing about the Amazon for twelve years, but Anapu was several days' hard travel from where I live in southeastern Brazil, and the Transamazon Highway had always seemed a journey too far—until July 2003, when I hosted two young students who wanted to film in the jungle and trekked up to meet her.

Barely eighteen months later she was dead, and as I heard her story, I became increasingly drawn to learn more, partly because I had never written a book about a woman, partly because there were parallels between her life and mine. Like Dorothy, I came from another country to Brazil. Like Dorothy, I found myself working on new ways of caring for forests and forest people, and like Dorothy, I believe that God is good.

This book makes no pretense of being a definitive biography. It is an investigation into Dorothy's life in the context of the violent land struggles in the Amazon. I started by paying a visit to her congregation in Cincinnati, Ohio, where I was graciously received and given an office and enough archival material to write a whole series of books. On my return to Brazil, taking advantage of the dry season, I set off to meet some of Dorothy's people and explore the issues that had moved her to live and die for the forgotten settlers of the Transamazon Highway. I traveled on foot, by dirt bike, truck, and riverboat, and sometimes I was lucky enough to go by plane. I interviewed dozens of people, transcribed hours of tapes, read piles of books and newspaper clippings, and spent days trawling the Internet. I walked along the rutted roads where Dorothy had walked, stayed with the sisters in Anapu, slept in her bed, and read the books on her bookshelf. I met and talked to members of her family as well as other members of her order. I attended the trials of the two gunmen and the intermediary. I lobbied with Dorothy's friends and supporters for justice for her and for the others who have died in the same struggle; I returned to see the sisters in Cincinnati; I made a host of new friends; and in the course of this quest I discovered that people across the world have been moved by the story. This, then, is my account of an extraordinary woman whose name was Dorothy Stang.

ONE

SISTER DOROTHY IN THE AMAZON

February 10, 2005

Lying on her bed, Dorothy pulled the mosquito net close around her and tried to prepare herself for sleep. She felt tired and old, and her back ached. She felt suddenly alone. And afraid.

She could hear Nelda moving quietly in the kitchen, brewing up one of her herbal teas. The house was unusually quiet. Dorothy's bag was packed, her papers and maps were all in order, and she knew it was important for her to sleep if she was to have all her strength for the days ahead. She would need to convince the isolated families deep in the forest that somehow all would be well and that what had happened to Luis and his family would never happen again. The federal secretary for human rights had given her his word. The Land Reform Agency, INCRA, had given her its full support. The police had promised protection.

"There they were, Tato's gunmen, laughing at us and saying they were going to kill us," Luis had told her, his face drained of color, his eyes wide. "Tato came into my *barraca* waving a gun and started shooting in the air. [A *barraca* is a small shack built of saplings, with a grass roof.] 'OK, let's get started,' he kept saying. I knew we were all going to die. And then one of the kids began to cry and he said, 'Look here, I'll give you one more chance. I'll be here at six in the morning and I don't want to see a soul in this house. No one. If you're not out of here, I promise you I'll kill everyone, men, women, and children. And I'll raze this place to the ground.'

"I don't know how we made it through the night. There they were—Rayfran, Eduardo, and a couple of other gunmen prowling around outside. Shining flashlights, shouting at me to come out and prove I was a man. Laughing, laughing. They must have been drunk. Built a big fire outside, and I could hear them shouting, 'Hey, little shack, we're going to burn you down. Hey, Luis, if you're a man, why don't you come on out and talk?' And finally I went to the door and I said to them, 'Look, guys, leave us in peace, won't you? We'll be out of here in the morning for sure. But in the meantime, can't you let us all get some sleep?'

"Shortly after that it came on to rain, and they ran in and took shelter in the *barraca* they'd built right alongside ours. But I knew they were itching to get on with the job. We all huddled together, praying for protection and for morning to come. I was quite certain we were going to be killed. Francisca and the children were crying and I told them to be quiet. Didn't want the gunmen to know that they'd scared us.

"None of us slept. Before it was light we looked outside and couldn't see anyone, couldn't hear anything, so we crept over to Dona Maria's house to talk to her and João. They'd seen everything, but their shack was on the other side of the road and Tato wasn't pretending that the land over there belonged to him. It was only our side of the road that he was claiming, even though the government had told us we could have it. By the time João was out of his hammock, Dona Maria had got the fire lit and was heating up the water for coffee. 'You'd better get some food inside you,' she told us. 'Never know what the day is going to bring.'

"Five minutes later Rayfran shows up at the door and he says, 'Where's Luis? Is he here?' And I say, 'Yes, I'm here.' So he says, 'All right, I'll give you till nine o'clock. I'm going to take a walk around, and when I come back, I don't want to see anyone in that shack of yours, OK?'

"Well, I knew they meant what they said. So I say to Francisca, 'Look here, I'll take you and the children to the next road and I'll come back.' And she says, 'No, Luis, if you stay, we're staying. If we leave you here alone, heaven knows what you might do, and they'll kill you for sure. If we're going to die, we'll all die together. But if you leave, we'll all leave.'

"So we're scurrying around and packing up our things, and all the children are carrying bundles on their heads, and then all of a sudden we're out of the *barraca* and walking away. The worst moment of my life. All that hard work, all for nothing. We left with what we could carry. And as we're walking down the track, there's Tato in his truck, smiling, smiling. That was the worst of all. Smiling at us, and not a thing we could do. I'd have killed him if I could. We hadn't gone very far when we heard the sound of the chainsaw and we knew they were knocking down the house. And then we looked back and saw smoke. They'd kept their promise."

It was a familiar story in the lawless backlands of the Amazon forest, where Sister Dorothy had chosen to spend the previous thirty years fighting for the landless peasants. Again and again families would turn up on her doorstep, tired after days of travel, clutching their pitiful possessions and hoping that she would find them a piece of land. Dorothy would always give them a bite to eat and a place to hang their hammocks. That afternoon she had been hunched over the kitchen table where all her dog-eared maps were spread out, penciling in the names of the new owners of each lot in the Esperança Project, when yet another ragged family had arrived to ask about land. Dorothy had welcomed them with her usual warmth, served them a dish of rice and beans, and promised the father, Chico, that she would make space in her truck for him and the children next morning to go into Esperança and find a plot of land. "Be here early," she told them. "I want to leave by six. We'll be holding a meeting with the settlers in the afternoon, and if it's raining, who knows how long it'll take us to get there?"

Again and again the settlers had moved into the forest, made their small clearings, built their shacks, and planted their crops. They had come from the dry lands to the east, and the only way they knew to cultivate the soil was by slashing and burning. But as the forest was cut and the red earth was exposed to the pitiless heat of the tropical sun and the relentless pounding of the equatorial rains, their yields had declined steadily, until they had been forced to move on. For thirty years the settlers had been moving west into the virgin forests, and for thirty years Dorothy had been accompanying them. In those far-flung Amazon lands, separated from the great cities of Rio de Janeiro, São Paulo, and Brasília by thousands of miles and hundreds of years, the poor had been abandoned, with no protection against adventurers who came to seek their fortune.

Dorothy believed passionately in justice; she believed in the rule of law; she even believed that the government would deliver on its promises to find land for the settlers. In recent months she had enlisted the aid of a few influential friends to back her in her lonely battle. Three days earlier she and Nelda had traveled together down the long muddy road to Anapu, where Nelda was to join the sisters. Despite the rigors of the journey, Dorothy had returned energized and full of hope. She had gone to Belém together with a small delegation from Anapu to tell the story of Luis and to publicize the plight of the settlers. She'd spoken to journalists and lawyers and held meetings with the federal secretary for human rights, the federal prosecutors, a state senator, representatives of the Land Reform Agency, and both civil and military police. Luis had told his story, and the police chief had sat there with his mouth open, declaring that it was just like seeing it all with his own eyes. Luis had nodded vigorously and said, "Yes, and if you don't do something, they're going to kill us. I'm telling you straight—there are going to be a lot of deaths."

Promises were made. The land where Luis had built his house was indeed part of the Esperança Project. Dorothy would be given the documents to prove it and police protection anytime she wanted. The secretary said that this state of lawlessness would no longer be permitted. The government would guarantee their safety.

Dorothy's plan for the weekend was to arrive on Friday afternoon, have a preliminary discussion with the settlers, and confirm the meetings for Saturday and Sunday. That would give time for word to get out to the families who lived farther away. She would show them the land titles from the government and explain that they had nothing to fear from the gunmen. She would explain the situation to Tato and ask him to tell Bida and Regivaldo and the others. Once they understood that the settlers had clear title, there would be no further problem. She felt sure of it.

It was cold and damp out in the forest, where a bunch of men sat in a small wooden shack huddled over a smoky fire. "Sodding rain," muttered one of them. "I wish to God it would stop."

"Sodding forest," said another. "Spooks me out sometimes. I keep hearing noises. Give me a smoke, someone, will ya?"

"I'm clean out," said a third. "Here, have a drop of the hard stuff instead."

Wordlessly the young man reached his hand for the bottle, tilted it, and took a deep draft of the raw spirits. "That's better," he said. "Keeps out the cold."

There was a companionable silence as they all gazed into the fire.

Suddenly there was a noise outside. The men jumped to their feet and the door was thrown open. "Hey, boys," said the newcomer as he stamped his feet and shook the rain out of his hair. "Is Eduardo here?"

"And if he is?" came a voice from a hammock in the corner.

"Well, if he is," said the newcomer, "you can tell him I have a deal for him."

"So what's your idea of a deal?"

The newcomer bent over the hammock, whispered into Eduardo's ear, and handed him something.

Eduardo straightened up and looked at the shiny revolver. He turned it over, weighed it in his hand, pointed it at his companions, and cocked it.

All his life he had enjoyed watching cowboy movies on the television. Not for him the baseball cap of the landless laborer; he preferred to wear a sombrero. When he agreed to leave his home state of Espírito Santo and come into the godforsaken jungles of the Amazon, he had done it with one very specific purpose in mind: he wanted land. Lots of it. Land planted with lush pasture, with herds of white cattle dotting the fields. He would be driving a brand-new pickup, the envy of the other ranchers, and raising a family of strong sons to work with him.

How exactly was he going to get from here, sharing a dilapidated shack in the middle of the forest with a bunch of peons, to there? Swinging gracefully out of his hammock, he palmed the gun and stuck it in his belt. It felt good, as if it belonged there. Reaching into his pocket, he extracted a cigarette, lit it, and inhaled deeply. He studied the men sitting around the fire telling bawdy jokes and laughing. "Rayfran," he called. "Come here, man. There's something I want to discuss."

Dorothy must have wondered what would happen if Tato and the others refused to listen. What if they, young men swaggering under the power of their weapons and the certainty that might was right, carried out their threats? What if there was a gunfight? The settlers were nervous, and they had been pushed to the limit. They had their hunting rifles and knew how to melt into the forest and dispatch an unwary gunman, leaving no trace. Despite the fine promises she had been given in the city, Dorothy knew that the land conflicts would not be solved by producing a bit of paper. There would be more violence, and she didn't know how to stop it. Was she wrong to be encouraging the settlers to hold out in the face of such appalling odds? What if the gunmen were to kill her? She took a deep breath and tried to face the possibility calmly, but her body betrayed her, and suddenly the tension of the previous weeks overcame her. Dorothy put down her head and wept.

There was a tap on the door, but Dorothy seemed not to have heard. Minutes later she opened her eyes and looked up into the anxious face of her only companion that evening, Sister Nelda.

"Whatever is the matter?" asked Nelda, concern shining out of her dark eyes.

"They are going to kill me," said Dorothy, suddenly calm. "I know they are going to kill me."

Nelda reached under the mosquito net for Dorothy's hand. What could she say? She had arrived in Anapu only three days earlier; she scarcely knew Dorothy, and she prayed desperately for guidance. "That's because the *senhora* is a saint," she said.

Dorothy smiled through her tears and squeezed Nelda's hand. The two women sat together in silence while the minutes ticked past. Dorothy sniffed and wiped her eyes with the edge of her sheet. "Don't worry, Nelda," she said, managing a smile. "Nobody would have the courage to kill an old woman like me."

Dorothy never noticed when Nelda stole softly out of the room. She turned on her side and slept.

Friday, February 11, dawned overcast and damp. Dorothy groped for the light switch and looked at her watch. Past five already, and hadn't she told everyone they'd be leaving at six?

Nelda was already standing at the stove and handed her some hot sweet coffee. Together they went into the front room and lit the candles in front of the image of the Virgin. Dorothy picked up her Bible and began to read the passage of the day.

Twenty minutes later she poured herself some more coffee and mentally reviewed the day. Collect the government food rations for the settlers. Check all her documents. Close up the house. Feed the cats. Stop at the police station to collect their escort. Remember to leave space in the truck for Chico and his family. Looking at her watch, she realized she still had a few minutes in hand. She went into her bedroom and put through a call to her brother David in Colorado.

She'd kept in close touch with David ever since he had paid her a visit a few months earlier, and he, best of all her family, knew how precarious the situation was. When he inquired after her, she could hear the concern in his voice. "I'm fine." She smiled. "Breathing in the cool fresh air. I feel better just talking to you." But when he pressed her, she told him that she was getting ready to go into Esperança, the place where they'd had all that trouble with people's houses being burned down and gunmen all over the place. "I can hear the people outside, waiting for me," she told him. "And I don't know why, but I'm feeling very nervous about it."

"Sister Dorothy!" As she hung up, Gabriel from the Farm Workers' Union walked into the kitchen and helped himself to coffee. "Are you ready? Time to go!"

"Good morning, Gabriel," said Dorothy, dialing another number. "I'll be right there. Just let me have a quick word with Felício."

Gabriel smiled. What an unlikely friendship, he thought—the white-haired American nun and the handsome young federal prosecutor from Belém. Over the past five years the two had become firm friends, almost like mother and son, although Felício described it as "love at first sight."

Felício was speaking from Altamira, where he was getting ready to join the federal environment minister and a government delegation on their flight to the small river town of Porto de Moz for the opening of the first extractive reserve in the area. (An extractive reserve is government land designated for extractive use by traditional forest populations, with the objective of preserving the environment through sustainable use of natural resources—rubber, nuts, wood, and so forth.) It was a project after Dorothy's heart, and Felício had done his best to persuade her to go along. But she had been resolute. The settlers were expecting her in Esperança, and she couldn't let them down.

When Felício remembered that conversation later, he realized that there had been something unusual about it. Dorothy was always one for getting to the point, he said. She didn't mince her words. But on that occasion she told him repeatedly not to worry about her, that she was going into the forest with a group of friends from the union and she wouldn't be alone. "She must have told me a dozen times not to worry about her," he said. "And then she said, 'Felício, don't ever give up, do you hear me? You have to keep up the fight. You mustn't give up and you mustn't abandon our people, do you understand? You must keep on fighting because God is with you.' She'd never spoken like that before."

"OK, Sister." Gabriel hoisted Dorothy's backpack, wondering for the umpteenth time how she could carry such a heavy weight. Dorothy picked up the cloth bag in which she carried her maps and her battered Bible, took a deep breath, and walked out into the morning rain. A handful of people were standing by the car, and the boxes were loaded. "Good morning, Ivan," she said, smiling at the young driver. "Are we all set? First stop, the police station, to pick up our escort, OK?"

Ivan nodded, checked that all his passengers were comfortably settled, let out the clutch, and drove cautiously off along the muddy road.

It was a few minutes after 6 A.M., and in the forest the rain had been falling steadily all night long. Rayfran pushed open the door of the wooden shack and looked out. "Sodding rain," he announced. "God, how I hate it!"

It was dark and gloomy under the cover of the tall trees, there were deep puddles on the road, and the men would willingly have wrapped themselves in their jackets, climbed into their hammocks, and gone back to sleep. None of them could be bothered to light the fire, and there was nothing to eat except a few pieces of cold, leathery meat. Eduardo felt cold and tired and hungover. Even the first cigarette of the day tasted sour. He thrust his feet into his boots, pulled on his jacket, and lurched to his feet. "Come on there, you lazy buggers," he growled to his companions. "Better get going—there's work to be done."

TWO

DAYTON DAYS

Dorothy Mae Stang, universally known as Dot, made her first appearance on June 7, 1931, the fourth of nine children born to a devoutly Catholic German-Irish family in Dayton, Ohio. It was a world that was on the one hand ordered and predictable and on the other unknown and scary, given the economic depression that had turned the world upside down, heralding a decade that grew increasingly turbulent until the world erupted into war.

Dot's father, Henry, was an officer at Wright-Patterson Air Force Base in Dayton, named for the pioneers of flight, Wilbur and Orville Wright. A summa cum laude graduate in chemical engineering from the

University of Dayton, he was an organic farmer at heart and would often differ forcefully with his colleagues, pounding the dinner table and saying that chemists were ruining Americans' food and their land. "Mom and Dad believed that God made the world and we should respect it," said their daughter Barb. "We'd never dare throw out an apple peel or a banana, and we composted before anyone knew what that was." Their mother, Edna, devoted her considerable energies to raising her nine children while keeping in touch with her large extended family, cooking huge meals, and somehow or other making ends meet in a situation where there was always homework to be done, clothes to be mended, and scraped knees to be kissed better.

Henry and Edna both came from large families: they were both the eldest of nine. A month before her marriage Edna's father died of pneumonia, but in his last days he told the young couple to go ahead with the wedding, since they were going to have to take care of the two families as well as their own children when they came. Edna's brothers lived up to their reputation as wild Irishmen and were described as "real rascals" who liked to drink and fight. Grandma McCloskey was caught in the middle, and many a time Edna would have to call Henry to sort out McCloskey family quarrels. But the boys had good hearts and often invited the Stang kids over to the family farm and plied them with chocolate drinks and bottles of milk to take home.

Not that Henry's siblings were much better behaved. A second-generation German family, they spoke German at home and German when they wanted to discuss private business. The eldest ones were girls, but the boys were a tough, hardheaded lot, and Henry quickly discovered that the only way to control them was by asserting his authority as the oldest. He treated his children with the same unwavering sense of justice and discipline, but underneath his stern exterior he too had a gentle heart.

The Stang family consisted of John, Jim, Mary, Dot, twins Maggie and Norma, Barb, and twins David and Tom. Mary was the enforcer. "She broke many a yardstick over our various body parts," Tom remembers. Dot, on the other hand, was both the primary caregiver (she used to get the little ones out of bed and ready for school) and the moral force who washed out David's mouth with soap the first time he used the F-word.

Life in the house at 5560 Markey Road was ordered by strict adherence to routine and stringent economic measures. The weekly routine included daily mass, school, homework, household and garden chores, fish on Fridays, weekly confession, choir practice, and the Saturday bath. It was a loving, safe, simple childhood—there were no such things as designer glasses, designer jeans, teeth being fixed. No school uniform—the kids wore T-shirts and long pants, and the smaller boys wore lederhosen until they went to school.

Tom describes the house as a place where all the boys and girls led devout Catholic lives and from which they evolved into many-splendored human beings. With so many mouths to feed, money was short, but Henry was nothing if not resourceful. Thrifty, capable, and exacting, he instructed his children to wash and save used cans, he carved soles for the family's shoes out of old tires, and he saved on the water bills by building a cistern to catch rainwater. Family members agree with Barb when she recalls that "Dad read the meters every day to record our us-

age of water and electricity," although there is some discussion about the extent to which they complied with the rule that prescribed one inch of water in the weekly bath. Money was always tight, and all the kids pitched in to help stretch the budget. The older boys had a paper route, and the younger kids worked summers picking fruit. Times were tough all around during the Great Depression, and it wasn't unheard of for people to kill themselves out of despair when they could no longer support their families.

The Stangs' was a self-sufficient lifestyle, isolated from the rest of the world, although they did hear news from far-off lands on the radio and see military planes flying overhead from the air force base, and in due course the older boys went off to war, John to be a pilot in Europe and Jim to join the navy in Alaska. Every night after supper the family huddled around the radio to listen to news about the war, particularly enjoying the rousing speeches of Winston Churchill. Among the family friends were several test pilots who lived close by, and the family remember being deeply affected when one of these dashing young men was killed.

The Stang children attended St. Rita's Catholic Elementary School and were constantly being reminded that they were Catholic while the rest of the world was other—probably

WASP (White Anglo-Saxon Protestant). Catholics were a minority in the area, but because of the size of their families they were not easily intimidated. Occasional disagreements with children from the public school—who by definition were not good Catholics—could result in a mutual exchange of rocks. Although fighting was not encouraged, it was a far less serious crime than disobeying household rules and regulations. Infractions had to be taken to Father Schmidt, whom all the children adored, and then later, during weekly confession, to Father LaMotte or Father Fogarty, both of whom they held in healthy respect. The venial sins of talking back, using bad language, and disobeying all needed to be confessed and forgiven, whereas more serious sins, such as missing Sunday mass, were unthinkable. Small offenses like raiding someone's piggy bank or fighting with a sibling were best forgotten, but penalties for getting caught were enforced by generous doses of castor oil, a good caning with a willow stick, and, for extreme offenses, being sent supperless to bed. This Catholic lifestyle was crammed with as many devotional practices as the church could devise, all focused on the Blessed Virgin or the Eucharist. Every morning began with mass, which involved fasting from the previous midnight. The communion wafers are considered to be the bread of angels, and if the consecrated host becomes stuck to the palate, under no circumstances can an unconsecrated finger be used to dislodge it. The Catholic message was reinforced throughout the school day, and after supper there was no question of running out into the yard for a ballgame before the family had gathered to say the rosary, a practice capped off with the Litany of the Blessed Mother and followed by the nightly tussle over the dinner dishes. High schoolers were excused from dishwashing, but the younger twins, David and Tom, were drafted for duty until they left to study at the seminary.

In retrospect, Tom recalls their universe as being "pretty narrow." The Jewish family next door was declared off-limits when the Stangs learned that their little kids had been seen wandering around stark naked during a New Year's Eve party. The Stangs' family friend and confidant Father Schmidt taught them to respect blacks, but Asians and Hispanics simply didn't enter their world. As for sex education, what little the boys picked up was gleaned from their monthly visits to the barbershop, where they could sneak a furtive look at the *Esquire* centerfolds of glamour girls. The barber's name was Windy Bill; he gave free haircuts to military personnel, and his conversation was peppered with sexual allusions and swear words not commonly used in the Stang household. Another fertile field for hearing ribald stories about women was the golf course, where the boys would caddy for rich businessmen whose conversation often revolved pleasurably around sex.

The big white wooden house, remodeled by Henry and the boys, was always open to family and friends to share a meal or find a bed if needed. Sharing what they had was part of the family ethos, and their generosity was frequently repaid. Dot's siblings have fond memories of one particular family friend who brought them a box of doughnuts every week.

The house was spacious, but none of the children had his or her own room. One bedroom was shared by Dot and Mary, and this was where Mary hid her piggybank and hung a Halloween skeleton on the wall. This combination proved too much for the twin boys, who would steal in to pry open the piggybank and move the arms and legs of the Halloween skeleton into scary positions, then retreat in gales of laughter. The second bed-room was shared by Maggie, Norma, and Barb. Their parents' room was off-limits, and when Tom illicitly entered, greatly daring, he found Henry's desk laden with books on organic gardening and home baking. He also discovered Henry's secret weakness: a passion for marshmallows. Tom and David shared the room that had previously belonged to Jim and John, strategically located next to the back staircase, which enabled them to make rapid getaways when necessary to avoid the wrath of their sisters.

The library was the place for homework and after-dinner games of chess, checkers, Monopoly, and Parcheesi. Edna always made sure to leave interesting books around, such as stories of the Holy Grail or the legends of King Arthur. It was here that she kept the statue of the Black Madonna of Prague, which she

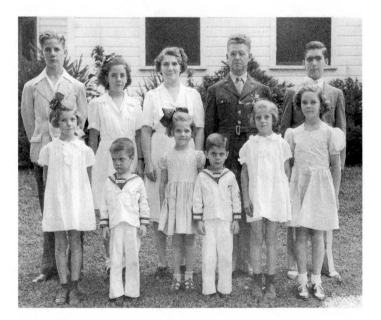

loved to decorate. There was no television, but there was an old-fashioned wind-up gramophone and the kids would sing along with the records, taking special delight in the musical *South Pacific*. Their favorite song was the one about Bloody Mary, and best of all was running around the house and yard belting out the final line: "Now ain't that too damn bad."

In the prevailing custom of the day, the sitting and dining rooms were reserved for church meetings and gala occasions such as the Fall Festival at St. Rita's Church and the annual picnic for St. Joseph's Orphans' Home. Both of these festivals were attended by hundreds of people; Henry was in charge of the gambling booth, and Edna presided over the kitchen. The kids remember having particularly delicious food on those occasions. On high days and holy days they would be roped in to put extra leaves into Grandma McCloskey's dining table so that it could accommodate twenty people and stretch into the sunroom. Festive meals would be topped off with Edna's wonderful desserts: shoofly pie, apple pandowdy, strawberry shortcake, pancakes with maple syrup, half a cantaloupe filled with ice cream. Edna's potato dumplings were immensely popular, but nobody cared for her liver dumplings. After dinner the older boys would argue the world scene with Henry while the little boys sat quietly on the bench and listened. At the slightest sign of fidgeting, Henry would give them one of his looks and they would be expelled from the room.

May was a festive month, particularly for the girls, with candlelight processions honoring the Blessed Virgin. They crowned her statue with flowers and sang "Bring Flowers of the Fairest." At the other end of the spectrum, the forty days of Lent were heavy with self-denial. All candy had to be kept in a special place and was usually given to the poor after Lent was over, although Tom remembers squirreling away candy bars for the Easter baskets. There were regular fast days (one square meal a day, with toast and black coffee for breakfast and peanut butter sandwiches for lunch) and a three-hour service on Good Friday with all the statues draped in purple. "By the time Easter came, with its brightly colored clothes and Easter eggs, we experienced a sort of resurrection from the dead ourselves," says Tom.

Henry especially loved the rituals connected with the festivals of the church. Every Christmas he strung the lights and made the family crèche, adding new touches year after year, and his beautifully crafted log cabin was the pièce de résistance on the table on Thanksgiving Day. Normally strict rules were relaxed on Halloween, when the kids were allowed to stay up until all hours collecting as much candy as they could carry—although they didn't always get to eat it. David has a clear recollection of their mother grabbing the bags, emptying the candy into a big box, and shipping it off to John and Jim to share with the troops who were fighting in the war.

Every spring Henry would oversee the preparation of the one-acre garden, which was fertilized so liberally with homemade compost and horse manure that it always produced a bumper crop of weeds, much to the dismay of the children. They were expected to plant and weed, pick and clean the vegetables and fruit, help Edna with the canning, and stack the cans in the basement. Sometimes they would go for walks with Henry and learn which mushrooms were good to eat, getting down on hands and knees and burying their noses in the warm, fermenting earth. "We had a sense of our hands being in the dirt. Smelling the sweet earth would tell us it was alive," says David.

Any surplus fruit or vegetables were sold at the roadside by the younger kids, which provided the household with a small extra income. In addition to the vegetables and fruit, there were chickens to be butchered and plucked, and in the fall bushels of walnuts had to be collected and shucked laboriously (with much banging of fingers) in order to extract the nuts for nutbread, leaving telltale yellowish oily stains all over the children's fingers. Firewood, hauled in from the air force base, had to be unloaded from the truck, chopped, and stacked in the boiler room so Henry could start the fire in the boiler, and the kids were expected to collect and sort the clothes for the ancient washing machine while taking special care to keep their fingers out of the wringer.

When school was out, the long hot summer days began at six o'clock sharp so they would be on time to catch the bus to Muma's Fruit Farm, where they picked strawberries and peaches until six o'clock at night—unless, miraculously, there was no fruit to pick and they were rewarded with a whole long day to get into trouble. Evenings provided an opportunity to play in the back yard, and as darkness fell they would collect lightning bugs in jars. When the violent thunderstorms of spring and early summer rocked the old wooden house, Edna would run around lighting candles to the statues of the Blessed Mother, sometimes prostrating herself on the floor to pray for protection for her family.

Winters in Ohio can be bitter, and the antiquated central heating system never did heat the upstairs bedrooms adequately. If a pane of glass in the window got broken, it didn't get fixed until spring. As ice formed on the inside of the windows and chilly drafts blew through the bedrooms, the kids snuggled under their heavy blankets and dreamed of ice-skating and falling snow. Tom and David would sometimes spray the driveway with water so they could skate at night down the hill to the river, and once they sledded down the driveway into the road without looking and were hit by a car. Fortunately, they were not injured, but Edna gave them a tongue-lashing to remember.

Once in a while John and Jim would come home for a visit, bringing their friends and telling great tales of heroic feats, real or imaginary. Jim had a Model T Ford he was inordinately proud of, and one can only imagine the harsh words he exchanged with Norma when she drove it headlong into a tree and almost destroyed it. When he left the navy, Jim presented the family with a mutt called Caledonia, who became a family favorite. On one occasion John put out a fire in the library, which might have burned the house down if he hadn't taken swift action.

People didn't travel very far in those days, particularly if there were so many bodies to fit into the family vehicle. But the family did sometimes get to the Forest Park Amusement Park or to the Stang cousins' family farm, and they went on excursions with the Inland Chorus. Choir practice was one of the highlights of the week, and the children acquired a wide repertoire, everything from operetta to old favorites. Mr. Westbrook, the choirmaster, even made a recording of the latest hits, which was sent to entertain the troops at the front, and some years later, when David entered the seminary, he recalled those songs as a solace in his loneliness. The boys of the Inland Choir wore Buster Brown outfits—black pants, short jacket, and shirt with a white collar—while the girls wore blue dresses with white collars and bows in their hair. On Saturday mornings the Stang kids had to do chores, but they tried their utmost to be through by noon so they could get to choir practice on time. They could take the bus, which cost them ten cents, or they could walk a couple of miles to the trolley, which cost three cents, leaving them money with which to buy candy or pop after choir practice. But when they did run late, Dot could often be relied on to figure out a solution and negotiate a ride with one of the neighbors heading for the grocery store.

Her siblings remember Dot as being a lot of fun. "She could make a game of anything," says her younger sister Barb. "She just bubbled. There was a lot of joy and happiness in the house when she was around." Not that she was a girly girl. She was the one who chose the players for the backyard ballgames, and the boys didn't argue with her because she was tough and gave as good as she got. "There were quite a few big families that lived on our street or nearby," Barb continues. "And there were fields and woods around the houses. The other families would have their little clubs and build clubhouses in the woods, and sometimes we would go over and burn their clubhouse down, and sometimes they'd burn ours down. And Dot was right there in the middle of it all."

Dot's sense of mischief often got her into trouble. She particularly enjoyed riding her bike, and one day when she was told to

practice piano she hid her bike
under the window. For a while
she pounded hard on the piano
keys, but then she climbed out
the window and pedaled away,
looking back over her shoulder
and laughing. All of a sudden
the front wheel hit a rock, and
she flew over the handlebars and
knocked out a front tooth. This
escapade ended with her dragging herself back to the house,
crawling back through the window, and doggedly reading the
music through her tears, with

blood in her mouth and the lost tooth perched on the piano.
Dot's best friend, Joan, recalls that throughout high school her
replacement tooth kept falling out and she would glue it back
with Elmer's Glue. Some sixty years later, on Dot's last trip to
Ohio, she was still looking around for glue to fix it.

This all-American life may sound like an idyll from a painting by Norman Rockwell, but life in the large family was a case
of survival of the fittest. The kids were fiercely competitive, and
Henry and Edna sometimes indulged in furious arguments, cul-
minating in Edna's packing her suitcase and disappearing for a
few hours. Separation or, worse, divorce wasn't really an option,
and after a few stormy hours life would resume its even tenor,
most probably, as Tom speculates, after Edna had had a good talk
with Father Schmidt. He instinctively understood the tensions
associated with living in a large family, and when things were

not going well he would sometimes appear with ice cream for everyone. Or he'd take the family out to eat, or off to the weekend camp at Top o'Hallow, where the kids could ride horses, swim in the river, and run around to their heart's content while the grown-ups played cards and Henry grumbled as he lost to his lucky Irish wife.

Naturally it was expected that several of the children from such a devout family would have a religious vocation; every family aspired to having at least one candidate for the priesthood, and if they could supply a daughter or two for the convent, so much the better. The two older Stang boys, John and Jim, enrolled in the seminary, but when the war came they went off to the service. The younger twins, Tom and David, both went to seminary and entered the priesthood, while first Dot and then Norma went into the convent, although Norma dropped out after making her temporary vows.

Dot's religious vocation was encouraged by the Sisters of Notre Dame at Julienne High School, where she and Joan threw themselves enthusiastically into caring for those less fortunate than themselves. Joan describes Dot as a woman who from her childhood knew that God loved her. Nourished in that love by her parents, her teachers, and her siblings, she grew into a woman of conviction, dedication, and sacrifice. The Sisters of Notre Dame taught that life's highest vocation was service to the poor, and Julienne girls collected money for so-called pagan babies abandoned on the streets of China and cared for by sisters from the same order. All the students at Julienne seemed so happy, Barb recalls. "There wasn't a Julienne girl who didn't think at some time about entering a convent."

A popular, athletic girl, always in the center of things, Dot was not above dragging her friend Joan to the school boiler room to sneak the odd cigarette. "She was mischievous, always ready to try something new," Joan recalls. But her deep spirituality was being well nurtured by the sisters. She was invited to join a club called Young Christian Students, where she and her friends met each week with their supervisor to pray, study the Bible, and figure out how they could be the yeast in the student body. The club had been started by a liberal cardinal who was criticized by some of his peers for producing student activists, and he certainly produced one in Dorothy. "The mission club was very strong in those years," Joan recalls, "and we learned about God's children in other lands, our brothers and sisters in Christ. And a desire began to grow and deepen in Dorothy's heart to give her life to God as a missionary. In those days there was something very romantic about being a missionary—going to missions and being a savior of the world."

It came as a surprise to nobody when Dot formally announced that she was planning to enter the convent. Henry wasn't happy when she told him of her decision. He figured that she was too young and hadn't seen enough of the world, but Dot's determination matched his, and on July 26, 1948, at the age of seventeen, Dot became a postulant in the order of Notre Dame de Namur and bounced joyously into her religious life.

THREE

ENTERING
RELIGIOUS LIFE

"What a big day that was." Joan laughs, recalling the day that she and Dot walked through the doors of the convent building at Mount Notre Dame in Cincinnati. "We were both very young—Dot had recently turned seventeen, and I was a few months older.

"We were very excited, and yes, a bit nervous too. The sisters welcomed us and took us off to change into our new black skirts and blouses. They gave us our postulants' caps and showed us how to attach them to our hair. After that we went out to say goodbye to our families. We had such mixed emotions—sad to part from our families and thrilled to be giving ourselves wholly to God. I think we thought that if we sacrificed everything, we would somehow become instant saints. I remember how disappointed we were when we got to the dormitories and found that we had beds to sleep on. Somehow I'd imagined sleeping on the cold floor!"

Liz Bowyer, who entered a couple of years later, describes the day she arrived at the convent: "I was in a kind of trance as I put my last cigarette out on the driveway. However, I was convinced that this was what God was asking of me."

The first thing they had to learn was how to walk like proper nuns, with hands folded and eyes downcast. At the same time they were adjusting to living in a community of over a hundred and fifty women and girls from different backgrounds, in poverty, chastity, and obedience, owning no personal possessions and having no best friends. This rule was designed to protect the girls from any relationships that might be considered unsuitable, but neither Dot nor Joan took it particularly seriously. They slept in dormitories with curtained cubicles containing a small nightstand, a basin with soap, towel, and washcloth, a "bed box" about 9 by 12 by 3 inches where they kept their white clothes (chemise, bib, headband, and bonnet) and a narrow bed with a straw mattress that had to be flipped every morning so it wouldn't sink in the middle.

They rose in silence in the chill of early morning (4:55 exactly, Joan recalls) and were expected to be in chapel by 5:30, in time for morning prayer, mass, and meditation. This was followed by breakfast—cornbread, fruit, and coffee—and then the day's work began, still in silence. All the women shared the chores. There was studying to be done, the rosary had to be recited, time had to be found for spiritual reading, and the sisters were sent in turn to help the cook prepare and serve the meals and clean up afterward.

By 11:45 they were back in the chapel to examine their consciences, and then they went to lunch—soup, meat or fish, vegetables, and stewed fruit. Water was the prescribed drink. No talking was permitted during meals, except on Sundays and feast days or occasionally when the superior felt that the community deserved a little extra recreation. Instead, one of the sisters would read aloud from a spiritual book. Conversation was allowed later, during the thirty-minute recreation period after meals, when they were encouraged to walk around in threesomes so that no sister would feel left out.

The afternoon's routine was much the same. From 5:30 to 6:00 they were back in the chapel for meditation, followed by supper, instruction, and recreation. Evening prayer was held in the chapel at 8 P.M. after which the sisters retired for the night. Baths were taken two or three nights a week, and although hot water was available, the sisters often took cold baths as an act of penance to mortify the flesh. At 9 P.M. the superior would knock on the floor with the heel of her shoe and the community would enter the Great Silence, during which any talking was strictly forbidden.

It was a lifestyle that required ample doses of self-discipline and dedication, and it must have been a hard adjustment for teenage girls who, despite the demands of school and family, had been enjoying a certain measure of independence. Dot and Joan did their best to conform to the model of well-behaved sisters, but underneath the habit they were still teenage girls. Joan remembers sneaking out behind the garage to the apple tree, where she would stay on guard while Dot shinnied up and came down with an armful of fruit, after which the pair would settle down in the grass, eating apples and chatting about their dreams for the future, silence or no silence.

One day Dot caught a snake and brought it into the house. The sisters waited until recreation time and then attempted to transfer it from a box to a jar. As it wriggled free, Dot was the first person out of the room. She held the door closed while the others ran around, with much screaming and laughing, to catch it and put it safely in the jar. Later that evening, during prayers, somebody started giggling, and soon the younger sisters were laughing uncontrollably. The superior gave them a sharp talking-to and sent them to bed.

Perhaps the hardest thing was being separated from their families. Liz recalls that the community was very strict about visits. These were permitted from members of the immediate family only once a month, on Sunday afternoons between two and four o'clock, and always took place in the auditorium, with no chance for privacy. The sisters were expected to write home regularly, but all incoming and outgoing mail was censored by the novice director. Phone calls were not allowed, and sisters could never go home, even if there was a death in the family.

There was so much to learn that the first six months passed quickly and soon the girls were ready to move on from the pos-tulancy to the novitiate. On January 26, 1949, with a shaven head and a brand-new habit, Dorothy Stang became a new crea-ture in Christ: Sister Mary Joaquim of the order of Notre Dame de Namur. Although some congregations made a big ceremony, inviting the family and dressing the novices as brides of Christ, the congregation of Notre Dame preferred a quiet ceremony with only the sisters present. "The hard part was having our hair cut off," says Joan. "But again, we were so excited about getting the habit that we accepted anything we had to." The superior of the province placed a white novice's veil on each girl's head, and Joan remembers being disappointed as she left chapel. She had thought that she'd suddenly be perfect, instead of which she could detect no difference except in her dress. The habit was made of black serge, with a big white bib, a white headband and bonnet that hid any trace of hair, and a waist-length veil. Both habit and headdress were fastened with pins, and many a time the girls inadvertently stuck themselves in their hurry to get dressed in time for morning chapel.

"Neither of us was best-dressed novice," Joan says with a laugh. "Of course there were no mirrors anywhere and we couldn't see what we looked like, so we always had something on crooked, especially when we were postulants. Dorothy used to charge into the kitchen to do the washing up in order to get a special grace, and sometimes her postulant's cap used to land in the dishwater."

It was quite a job managing those heavy habits. "We had two black habits, one for weekdays and one for Sundays," says Liz. "Every Sunday we would air out the weekday habit and brush out the dust. The bib, the headband, and the undergarments were numbered and washed by hand every week in the laundry. Every six months we dismantled the black habits and washed them out. They were terribly hot and heavy in the summer."

"I don't think we felt like brides of Christ as novices," adds Joan. "We were trying hard to learn how to pray, how to act, and how to be good Sisters of Notre Dame so we wouldn't be sent home."

"The bride image didn't have much appeal for me," says Liz.

"But I did feel very much in love. I think that the best part was being formed in prayer and educated for mission. All the sisters were our mentors, and there was something tremendously exciting about being part of a community dedicated to doing God's work. Our director was a wonderful woman who taught us what it meant to be in personal contact with God. I had a sense of giving of myself unreservedly. Chastity? Up to the first vows, that was especially hard. I still had some tough times after that, but those early days were the most difficult. Poverty wasn't really an issue. We had to ask for anything we wanted, like soap, toothpaste, that sort of thing, but we never lacked for anything. I always had what I needed, and I learned some conservation habits that I should be practicing today. I did bring a dowry to the order—my last two paychecks, about sixty dollars. The order never made much money on me! Bills were paid from sisters' stipends. I don't know how they made ends meet. Of course, doctors gave discounts and education bills were low. As for obedience, our directors were basically sensible women, so they didn't ask us to do things that were unreasonable."

Joan agrees. "Obedience was not usually too hard. Everyone was doing the same thing. Although sometimes our director used to ask us things just to test us. Poverty wasn't too hard either, because we didn't go anywhere or do anything. What was difficult sometimes was that we had to ask for everything and we couldn't have anything beyond what was necessary for survival. We had no pocket money. If we had to take a bus, we were given the bus fare and that was all. We weren't allowed to own anything, and if we received gifts, they were handed in to the superior for the community to use.

"Chastity, on the other hand, is a great gift and a great struggle. I believe the vow of chastity takes on real meaning when we reach our thirties and see our friends and siblings with their families and we realize that we will never have a family of our own. The gift is that we are free to do God's work, never having to worry about being responsible for someone else. When Dot was in Brazil, she always used to say that she was free to speak out against injustice because she didn't have a husband or children who might be endangered and she knew her congregation would back her work with the poor.

"It is hard to remember what we missed most, but I would think it was communication with our families. We had a great time and enjoyed one another. We actually liked what we were doing, for the most part! Christmas Eve mass was like entering heaven. The chapel was beautifully decorated, and Christmas carols were played for an hour before midnight mass. We had sisters who played the organ and violin and one who played the cello. The music was so glorious that we used to think we had died and gone to heaven."

Liz agrees. "I guess my first Christmas in the convent was a piece of heaven. Entering chapel with all the beautiful decorations and candles and listening to the sisters playing that wonderful music was a very moving experience.

"Clothing days—when we got the habit—and vow days were always special, because they signified one more step toward our goal of giving ourselves completely to God. Even holy days were special. We had extra-nice desserts and were allowed to talk during meals."

"We weren't allowed to have special friends," Joan continues. " 'Particular friendships,' as they were called, were frowned upon. I remember being told that every time I talked to one of the sisters, I was to imagine I was meeting a princess for the very first time—can you imagine that?

"We did have a priest who acted as our chaplain and said mass for us every day. In the forties and fifties, until Vatican II, nuns were looked down upon as second-class citizens in the church and servants to the priests—and there are still some priests today who hold this view! However, Julie, our founder, believed wholeheartedly in our autonomy and taught us to be strong women.

"We went to confession once a week, made an eight-day retreat once a year—we still do—and never ate in front of anyone who was not a religious. When we did anything wrong, we told the superior, and she would give us a penance to say, and that would be the end of it.

"We didn't listen to music or go to the movies or watch TV. Our reading was confined to spiritual books and those textbooks we needed for our studies, and our days were so full that we didn't have time to think about anything else."

"We knew very little about what was going on in the world," adds Liz. "We read newspaper clippings of selected articles, and the first time we watched television was at the funeral of President Kennedy. We studied on Saturdays and during the summer, and it took me ten years to get my degree. Since we were a teaching order, I taught for eight of those ten years, but I always had excellent mentors. My area of concentration didn't take much discernment—one day on the way out of the dining room the directress of studies said to me, 'English for you.' "

So why would any teenage girl want to abandon friends and family, submit to such harsh conditions, give up her chances to marry and carve out a life for herself, and bind herself to uncon-

ditional vows of poverty, chastity, and obedience? Why, in the
1950s, when America was entering the golden age of apple pie
and motherhood, rock and roll and fish-tail Cadillacs, would a
young girl want to shut herself away from the big world and become a teacher in a parish school? And if she wanted to love
and serve God, why join this particular order?

No doubt it was because of what Dot and Joan had seen
at Julienne High School among the Sisters of Notre Dame de
Namur—women with hearts as wide as the world telling the
love of God.

The order was founded by a pair of friends, Julie and
Françoise, during the turbulent times that followed the French
Revolution. Religious education had been abandoned during
the violent changes that followed the overthrow of the old
regime, and the two women felt that what France and her people needed above all was to love and follow the good God. Since
1804, when the order was founded, thousands of women from
across the world have joined in this mission, setting up schools
on five continents. Their calling is based on the simplest of be-
liefs: that God is good. "Ah, how good is the good God!" was an
exclamation constantly on Julie's lips, and across the world today the congregation of Notre Dame echoes the good news of
God's goodness. God is and has been in all creation since the beginning of time, God's creation is good, and God knows how to
make everything turn to the good of those who love God with
all their hearts and who put their trust in God.

Julie taught that those who put their trust in God will never
be shaken, whether by criticism or by opposition. They will be
courageous, simple, carefree, and joyful. They will take their
stand with everything that brings and nourishes life, they will

work to befriend, support, and empower all of God's creation, and they will have a special heart for the poor. Julie wrote, "We exist only for the poor, only for the poor, absolutely only for the poor," and years later the order refined this to give special priority to the worst victims of poverty: women and children.

Since the days when Dot and her friends had collected money for the poor children of China, Dot had nurtured a desire to be a missionary. She and Joan used to dream of doing something wonderful for God and often discussed it, over sodas at school and over the illicitly picked apples at the convent. Together they plunged into their religious education, working, studying, and dreaming of the day when they could go out and make a difference in the world. But their future lay not in China, which was closed to Christian missionaries, but in another country altogether, and they were to spend many years learning to live among the poor before reaching the mission field where God had destined them to work.

Three years after entering the convent, on January 27, 1951, the two friends made their first vows. The white veils of novices were replaced by the black veils of professed sisters as they pledged themselves to God and to the community for one year. Kneeling at the communion rail, they each held a candle as they pronounced their vows. Every member of the community came up in turn to welcome them, and so they passed from novices to professed sisters. The sisters would renew their annual vows twice in the following two years, then for a period of three years, and finally forever.

Six months after making her first vows, at age twenty, Dot was sent to teach third grade in a parish school in Calumet, Illinois. A few months later she transferred to another school, where she taught fourth and fifth grades. After two years in Illinois she was judged ready to move on, and so she took her first steps on the path that was to lead, years later, to the Amazon forest of Brazil. Together with three other sisters, she was sent to Arizona, and there it was that she discovered her true vocation: calling forth the gifts of God's children and helping them to raise themselves out of poverty.

FOUR

FIRST STEPS
IN MISSION

Dot's early years in the convent passed quickly amid the
many things she had to learn: how to live in community, how to nourish her spirit through prayer and reflection, how to adopt the disciplines of poverty, chastity,
and obedience, how to separate herself from attachment
to worldly things, how to value and get along with each
member of her congregation, and how to become a perfect servant of God. If there were moments of doubt and
despair, we never hear of them. What we see is a woman
moving steadily along her appointed path and preparing
herself to be of service to God and to the world.

After five years, when she had just turned twenty-
two, Dot was considered by her spiritual directors to be

ready to start her life's work. She had served her apprenticeship in parish schools in Illinois, and now it was time for her to fly farther from the nest and move across the country to teach in the brand-new parish school of the Most Holy Trinity in Phoenix, Arizona.

She arrived with three members of her congregation—Sister Ann Timothy, Sister Paula Marie, and Sister Angelina—on a boiling hot day in August 1953, and the first thing that struck her was the intense dry heat of the Arizona desert. "It was un-believably hot," says Paula Marie, "and the traditional black habits and veils we wore were very uncomfortable in that cli-mate. They used to get covered in dust because of the constant dust storms. I remember that the school was built right in the middle of a grapefruit grove. We had irrigated land all around us, but the school grounds were tremendously dry and dusty, and I remember the tumbleweed rolling through the playground. Later we changed our habits to gray and replaced our black veils with white ones. That was a big improvement."

The four sisters were to staff the entire school from grades one through six. Dot and Paula Marie were both twenty-two, Ann Timothy was twenty-eight, and Angelina was forty-five.

Their house wasn't yet ready to be occupied, so during those first weeks they stayed with the Good Shepherd Sisters, who had a traditional convent and a boarding school for girls who were wards of the state. But work on their house progressed fast, and it wasn't long before they were able to move in. Their new home consisted of two prefabricated houses joined together and was located right next to the school. After the large, impersonal convents they were used to, they must have felt like a little fam-ily in their new house, and the parishioners did what they could to make it friendly and welcoming. "It was a great experience for us to live in such a close-knit situation," says Paula Marie. "And the parishioners became an important part of our lives in those early years."

The priests at Most Holy Trinity had come from Ireland as missionaries. "They were wonderful, energetic, and very zealous in spreading God's kingdom," recalls Paula Marie. "And they had a great sense of humor. The pastor, Father Neil McHugh, used to take us out on day trips to show us the natural beauty of Arizona. It was all so new and unfamiliar to us. We had a great relationship with the priests. They recognized our gifts and gave us a lot of freedom to accomplish our work."

The sisters felt a new independence in being so far from the mother house in Ohio. "It was a great place to be," remembers Paula Marie, "especially since at that time there was a lot of turmoil in the church and religious life because of all the changes taking place as a result of the Vatican II council."

The Second Vatican Council was called by Pope John XXIII from 1962 to 1965 to enable the Roman Catholic Church to redefine its priorities. Vatican II, as it was known, formalized a movement that had been slowly growing as some members of the church began to reevaluate their whole way of being and living as followers of Christ. Known as liberation theology, this new thinking held that the Kingdom of God was here and now and that God's people were to work for social and political freedom and justice. Parishes were divided up into groups of laypeople known as base communities, where the emphasis was placed on empowering the laity to study the Bible, reflect on their day-to-day lives, and act in accordance with the liberating truths of the Gospel. Priests and nuns were abandoning both the Latin mass and their traditional dress. Inside church buildings, priests turned to face the people during the mass, inviting them to celebrate God's feast together, instead of turning away from the people to face God. The church was slowly relinquishing its absolute hold on power and was placing itself on the side of the poor and powerless.

"We had to completely rethink how to be a church in the changing world," says Paula Marie. "It was tremendously exciting." The sisters still observed the rule, held private and community times of prayer, attended daily mass, and tried to keep at least some time for silence and reflection. They also observed their vows of poverty, chastity, and obedience. "The vow of poverty was the same as it had been in Ohio," says Paula Marie. "Pretty much like what we were used to, since all things are held in common—we do not own things and are accountable for community money we spend. And of course we all shared in the ordinary chores of cooking, cleaning, and so on."

Their community belonged to the Ohio Province, and even though they had complete autonomy in the conduct of their everyday affairs, they were responsible to and accountable to the provincial (the superior of the province). The provincial used to pay an annual visit to each house to meet with the community as a whole and with each sister individually. The sisters also received visits from the educational supervisor, who observed their teaching and offered suggestions for improvement. So they felt still very much a part of the Ohio community, even though the distance meant that they didn't see much of their birth families except on visits back to Ohio. "My family came twice during my six years in Arizona, so I did get to see them," Paula

Marie remembers. "And every family visit to one of us was a visit to all of us and a very special occasion."

In 1956, three years after her arrival in Arizona, Dot went back to the mother house in Cincinnati to join a group of other young sisters preparing for their final vows. She stayed for six weeks and returned a fully professed sister, at the age of twenty-five.

Life in Arizona revolved around the parish hall, where Sunday masses were held, the little chapel of Our Lady of the Wayside, and the school. As time went by, the parishioners managed to build a church and expand the school building. The sisters must have been good teachers and popular with the children, because by their second year they had seventy students crowded into their classes. There was such demand that they added a new grade every year: first seventh and eighth grades, then a kindergarten, and then they finally had to split some of the grades in two. Dot and Paula Marie were fortunate enough to be able to teach the same group of children over a four-year period, changing grades with the children as they moved up. "It was an unusual arrangement," says Paula Marie, laughing, "but it had a lot of advantages. We got to know the children and their families well and formed lasting bonds with them."

Not only did they know the children from four years together in the classroom, but they also shared parish life with their families. Of course, there was one large group that had no access to religious education, and that was the kids who attended public school. The sisters resolved to provide instruction for those who were interested, and before long any spare time was taken up with extra classes in religious education: Saturday mornings for grades one through eight and Wednesday evenings for high schoolers.

It was the priests who encouraged the sisters to move beyond the parish boundaries to work with the children of Mexican migrant laborers and Navajos. The Mexicans came to work in the lettuce and cotton fields and would stay for several months, until the harvest was over, when they would move on. Some of the families returned year after year, and when the children weren't working in the fields, they attended the local public schools. Children learned English, but their parents spoke very little.

Dot loved nothing better than to hitch up her habit, call Paula Marie and Ann Timothy, and jump into the battered old parish station wagon to head for the one-room shacks where the dark-eyed children were waiting. Angelina wasn't often able to

join them since she was so busy at the school, but she strongly encouraged the sisters and visited when she could, and sometimes the assistant priest, Father Joe, went along for the ride.

"Spanish?" Paula Marie laughs. "We did pick up a little Spanish, but most of the Mexicans could understand and speak some English, and they were certainly better with English than we were with Spanish! Dot was probably the best among us, but she could communicate very well without having a good command of the language."

Conditions in the migrants' camps were always precarious and often downright unsafe. The houses were tiny and cramped, and there was neither running water nor electricity. But the families were close and did what they could for their children. They may not have attended church very often, but they considered themselves Catholics and were punctilious about sending the children for Friday afternoon instruction with the sisters.

"Our classroom was the outdoors," says Paula Marie. "It was the only place with enough space! But it worked out fine because the weather was so beautiful. Sometimes the families would drag out a bench or a couple of chairs, but if not we could always sit on the ground. What we wanted to do was teach the children some elements of their faith and show them how important they were to us and to each other. Of course we learned more from them than they did from us!"

The sisters tried to explain to the parents that if the children worked long hours in the fields, they'd be too tired to attend school, and every child had the right to be in school. They also talked about health and the dangers for young children of being around when the crops were being sprayed. They told the children that they were part of the church family, special and valuable children of God, and that the other church members cared deeply about them. This contact with the migrant families made the sisters increasingly aware that social justice was an arm of education and the two couldn't be separated, and when they looked back on this period, they reflected that they had been doing liberation theology, even if they didn't call it that.

They also encouraged the parish members to share what they had with these migrant families, setting up a place in the school where people could leave gifts of food and clothing. They prepared the children for their first communion and always managed to get hold of the most beautiful white dresses and veils for the girls and dress suits for the boys. On the great day, the families would turn out to admire the children as they walked solemnly in procession, dressed in all their finery. The mothers would come inside the church, but the fathers always stayed outside—except on Good Friday, when the sisters used to throw a party in the afternoon and invite everyone inside to select whatever clothing or food they wanted. It was important to have new clothes for Easter, and it was a revelation to the sisters to see that none of the Mexicans took more than they needed. They chose very carefully and often shared with others.

"Friday afternoon was our time for going out to the camps," says Paula Marie, "and later on we started working with the Navajo Indians as well. There's one family that I remember to this day. It consisted of the father, some older brothers, and one younger boy, whom I taught. They lived in a one-room house with a dirt floor and a small lightbulb hanging from the roof. There wasn't any running water, and they had to get water from the standpipe and use the outside privy. I'd never seen poverty like that before, and it made a profound impression on me. Of course our main focus was on religious education, but we did what we could to help out if they needed anything, and sometimes they'd seek us out in town if they were in any sort of trouble."

Dot's brother David remembers driving down with his parents from Ohio to visit her and how she would beg them to pick her up after school and head for the migrants' camps. "She'd hug the kids and knock on the doors, and the men would be out working or drinking and so she related to the women and kids."

Nine years later, in 1964, when Sister Mary Jeanne joined the group, it had grown to eleven and Dot had become the superior. By that time the sisters were living in two houses. One of them contained a small chapel as well as space for eating and living and accommodation for six of the sisters. At the end of the day the other five would walk across the road to sleep in the cramped house that had formerly belonged to the parish priest. Private study was done either in the main house or in one of the school classrooms.

By this time the school had grown enormously. "There must have been around five hundred children when I arrived," Mary Jeanne recalls. "Each grade was divided in two, and I believe there was a sister for each grade. There were also a lot of lay teachers. It was a very nice school—it had a great atmosphere, largely due to the sisters. Dot was both school principal and superior of our little community. One of the things I remember most about Dot was how cheerful she always seemed. I don't know if she really wanted to be principal deep down, but she certainly did a great job."

Because Paula Marie and Dot had not completed their education, they tried to carve out some time on Saturday afternoons to study, and every summer they would spend six weeks at the College of St. Joseph on the Rio Grande in Albuquerque, New Mexico. It was a new college, serving both religious and laypeople, and the sisters took a variety of liberal arts, science, and education courses, which they felt gave them a good grounding for their work. Paula Marie later completed her degree in Ohio, and Dot finally completed hers in 1964, at the age of thirty-three, at the College of Notre Dame in Belmont, California.

The first years in Arizona were very busy ones. "We were young and our energy levels were high—which was just as well!" reflects Paula Marie. "During all the years out there, the school was our original and full-time mission, but we did manage to do a lot of other things as well. We absolutely loved those early years! We had such fun, so many adventures. It was really an invigorating time for us. And we learned so much. Everything that we did seemed to enrich everything else, and had such an impact on our future lives.

"I think for Dot the Arizona years led her to push forward in a strong desire to work with the marginalized and the poor, and certainly laid the foundation for her future work in Brazil. We all moved on to different locations and jobs, but the bonds we formed were lifelong. Whenever Dot returned to Ohio from Brazil, we never missed getting together and sharing what was going on in our lives."

In December 1964, an article appeared in the *Arizona Republic* describing the sisters' work with the migrants. Dot, still known as Sister Mary Joaquim, is described as "a ball of fire. A tiny woman with an enormous soul, she wanders among 'her families' in soothing gray garb and flowing white veil, chatting one minute and dispensing discipline the next. The light, care and determination that pour out of Sister Mary's eyes almost make her a fire hazard, and already many blazes have been kindled in many heads. For the children she is there as teacher. For the families she and her Sisters become the church as they live out the gospel of Matthew 25: 35–41.

> For I was hungry and you gave me something to eat, thirsty and you gave me something to drink, I was a stranger and you invited me in, I needed clothes and you clothed me, I was sick and you looked after me, I was in prison and you came to visit me.
>
> Then the righteous will answer him, Lord, when did we see you hungry and feed you, or thirsty and give you something to drink? When did we see you a stranger and invite you in, or needing clothes and clothe you? When did we see you sick or in prison and go to visit you?
>
> The King will reply: I tell you the truth, whatever you did for one of the least of these brothers of mine you did for me.

"Did the families need food?" the article continued. "Sister Mary found some for them. Did a family of nine, living in an old bus, need a place to stay? She would try to find one. Did mothers who pulled their small babies in cartons through the cotton fields as they worked need blankets and baby clothes? Sister Mary Joaquim knew there had to be some somewhere and she would find them."

In the years to come, the Second Vatican Council and the Council of Medellin (a meeting of Latin American bishops to define the new theology) would radically change many aspects of the church. Dot was to live fully through those turbulent years, in which some priests and nuns would abandon the church altogether, some would fall back on the comforting familiarity of the old traditions, and others would cast off their habits and experiment with new ways of living in or outside communities.

In this work with the poor, Dot was getting basic training in her calling. In 1966 her heart's desire of being a missionary was finally granted, and she was sent, together with her friend Joan, to Brazil. She could have had no better preparation than those years in the migrant camps of Arizona.

FIVE

EARLY DAYS
IN BRAZIL

The sisters arrived in Brazil in August 1966, during the first years of the military dictatorship.

Their first intercontinental flight on the Pan Am plane took them from Miami to Rio, attended by petite, smiling air hostesses in hats and heels and trim suits. The plane swooped over the granite mountains and down over the great expanse of Guanabara Bay, delivering them to the chaos of the airport, the unfamiliar sounds of the language, the hassle of rounding up their luggage and clearing customs. Their senses must have reeled when they saw Rio de Janeiro, the Marvelous City, with its dazzling colors, the smell of the sea air mixed with those of sweat and sewage, the humid heat of the tropics. Christ the Redeemer with arms outstretched to embrace the city. Copacabana beach, with its sidewalks patterned in swirling black and white. People with skins of all shades, from palest café au lait to burnished black, the rich and sophisticated, the poor and hungry.

Rio offered a staggering contrast between rich and poor. Drivers skidded through the streets, hooting wildly and weaving through dense crowds of pedestrians, scooters, horse carts, and the occasional donkey. During violent storms, the thunder crashed around the mountains, but in the mornings the bay sparkled, its water the most delicate shade of turquoise, echoed and intensified by the deep blue of the sky and the glaring white sand of the beaches. The sisters must have been struck by a medley of impressions: street children, drunks sleeping on the sidewalks, military police in dark glasses, pickpockets, coconut sellers, street vendors; the noise that assaulted their ears; the rice and beans that were the staple diet; the scalding hot, viciously sweet little cups of coffee; the exotic fruits, mangoes and avocadoes, pineapples and bananas—fruits that looked like tomatoes, tasted sugary sweet, and were called persimmons; soft white cheeses; syrupy desserts.

Eventually the sisters piled into a car that took them on a winding road through exuberant forests to Petrópolis, in the cool mountains. Bobby, Patricia, Marie, Dot, and Joan, five sisters in habits from the ordered world of North America, soon found themselves in the mission training school that some of the great theologians of the time had passed through—Ivan Illich, Dom Hélder Câmara, Gustavo Guttiérez. They plunged into their new life with passion, attending Spiritist services and visiting the backyards of the Afro-Brazilian cults *macumba* and *umbanda*, where women whirled around the floor to the insistent sound of the drums and collapsed into trances when visited by the ancient gods of Africa. They studied liberation theology, the politics of resistance and history. Any thoughts that Spanish would see them through vanished like morning mist as they tried to get their unpracticed tongues around Portuguese, the "language of angels," with its nasal sweetness and its strange sounds that may have reminded them of the Polish still spoken in some areas of the Midwest.

There was so much to learn, so many new faces from all over the world, a wilderness of languages, experiences, stories to tell and hear, new ideas to be considered. To celebrate graduation from mission school they took a two-week trip around the colonial towns of Minas Gerais, where sweet-faced Virgins gazed down from ornately carved ceilings in gloriously gilded Baroque churches.

When it was time to set off for the mission field, the first leg of their journey took them to the decaying port city of Recife. As the sisters gathered their luggage and waited for the official signal to board the small plane, the other passengers surged on, leaving them with one seat facing backward and a couch in the tail of the plane. Some of the passengers started throwing up as the plane plunged and bucked through the turbulence, and the hostess ran back and forth passing out little bags and finally laying out newspapers on the floor.

When they finally landed in Recife, they were driven to visit the Sisters of the Blessed Virgin in the sixteenth-century town of Olinda. It must have been a blessed relief after their flight, and their eyes must have feasted on the view over the sparkling blue ocean dotted with rafts skimming over the water as the wind caught their patched sails. But the sisters were anxious to get on, and after a couple of days they took another small plane to the colonial city of São Luis, where they were warmly welcomed by the congregation of Notre Dame located on the outskirts of the city, in Rosário. There they spent their first tropical Christmas—a time to reflect once more on their upcoming mission and to thank their good God for bringing them safely so far from home.

The day after Christmas dawned with the arrival of the parish jeep from Coroatá, driven by a man named Braguinha. Bidding farewell to Marie, who was to stay in Rosário, the sisters piled themselves and their belongings on board and set off excitedly for the interior. It was a long, hot, dusty drive over corrugated roads, and twice the jeep bumped to a halt so Braguinha could change a wheel. As night fell, they finally arrived in the little town of Coroatá, to be welcomed by the bishop and the two young Italian priests, Lorenzo and Gabriel.

The sisters had stopped using the habit while in mission training. They were now dressed in black skirts and white blouses, and on the dusty journey they had taken off their veils in order to keep them clean. Their plan had been to put them on when they arrived, but much to their surprise, the bishop was delighted to see them without veils and told them so. They never wore them again.

Coroatá, Maranhão, a small town a long day's journey from São Luis, consisted of three cobbled streets and a maze of connecting side streets with open drains where children and dogs chased each other through the dust. The main square with the parish church was in the center of town, and the sisters' house was close by. The town was connected to the big world by a railroad and the dirt road to São Luis, and the townspeople made their living from subsistence agriculture—and from the *babaçu* nuts that grew so abundantly on the graceful palm trees in the fields. The women collected them, placed them between their bare feet, and sliced the tough husks with practiced strokes of their machetes before selling them to the landowners, who shipped them off to be processed into oil. It was grindingly hard work. The people were dirt poor, and they suffered from the diseases of poverty: worms and gut cramps, chest colds aggravated by the smoky woodstoves, malaria and tropical fevers. They treated their sicknesses with medicinal herbs and muttered prayers, and as a last resort they might consult the one doctor in town. He never got rich, because nobody had any money; he was paid in chickens or vegetables, or sometimes a leg of pork. Later on he became mayor, and then he left the town.

The sisters were given a pleasant, pink-washed adobe house with a tile roof. It had an erratic supply of running water, and the electricity, supplied by the town generator, was turned on between six and ten each evening so that the children could go to school, the only time they could set aside from work. The house was sparsely furnished: each of the nuns had a hammock, and there were a few chairs, a kerosene refrigerator, and a small gas stove, but they had no cooking utensils except for one battered skillet. Fortunately their mother general had provided them with some plastic plates and cups.

Maranhão was (and remains) a feudal state controlled by a few families of landowners and politicians. Here most of the people were considered fit only to till the soil and tend the cattle, and lived in submission to the boss, the priest, and the mayor. Children were expected to obey their parents without question, women to defer to and care for their men, and everyone to support the hierarchy, which benefited only the very few at the top.

"We color-washed our house and planted flowers, and after days of scrubbing and painting we were ready for open house and the bishop's visit," Joan recalls. "During mass the bishop called us to the sanctuary and asked us to say a few words. Dot was the appointed representative, and she had to think fast, but in her hour of need her Portuguese failed her and all she could say was 'Thank you, we're happy to be here, thank you very much.' Fortunately, the bishop rescued her."

Joan remembers their first visitor to the house: seventeen-year-old Gracinha, who dropped by to bid them welcome.

"I was born and raised in Coroatá," Gracinha says. "My parents were very old-fashioned, and I was a real rebel. All I wanted to do was wear miniskirts and listen to the Beatles, but my mother wouldn't hear of it. I couldn't even go dancing! We'd heard there were some foreign nuns arriving, so of course we expected a bunch of old ladies in black habits carrying crucifixes. And what did we get? Four thoroughly modern young women who seemed to be perfectly normal. And they were always so cheerful. Dorothy in particular was always smiling. She radiated peace and contentment.

"I was their first visitor. I said to them, 'Look, I live in this town and I wanted to come and welcome you.' They didn't speak Portuguese very well, and they needed to buy some things for the house but didn't know the words. I remember they were after a grinder for meat, but I hadn't the first idea what they wanted. Finally they just drew me a picture and I understood at once!"

The sisters chose Dorothy to be responsible for the household.

"She was always a very simple person," Gracinha says. "She wasn't the least bit vain. She always cut her hair really short so it wasn't a problem to keep it tidy. I used to laugh at her because she'd say she couldn't stand to have shoes on her feet, it had to be sandals. She used to leave home in the morning after prayers in the chapel, and she'd pray that Jesus would illuminate her so she could work with the poor and make their lives better.

"One day I happened to drop by when it was Dorothy's turn to do the cooking. And when I came in she said, in her funny Portuguese, 'Hey, Gracinha, look what I've been given.' It was a local fruit called *bacuri*. It's got a hard outer shell, so you crack it open. The flesh is white and a bit glutinous, and some people don't like it, but I think it's wonderful. That's the part you eat, but of course Dorothy didn't know that. And what do you suppose she'd done? Thrown out the seeds and the flesh, taken the shell, and tried to boil it up with water!

"The sisters didn't behave like traditional nuns," Gracinha continues. "So we didn't quite know what to make of them at first. It took us all a little time to settle down. They didn't even look like proper nuns. They didn't wear the habit. They wore skirts and blouses."

"We'd cut up our habits and made skirts," Joan confirms. "We'd made white blouses and black skirts, and we wore black hose and granny shoes—black lace-ups. We looked like idiots. People couldn't understand how we could have white faces and black legs—the kids kept trying to touch us! And of course we had to do without the veil. That was a saga in itself.

"The bishop explained to us that the local women just loved

63

to wear veils to mass. Well, they didn't all have a veil, so what they used to do was take a sheet or a tablecloth, and when they knelt at the altar for communion, they'd line up and get under it. But that sheet never quite covered everyone, and the ones on the end were always trying to tug it away from the others so they'd be covered! He wanted us not to wear the veil so the women would understand that it was OK not to have their heads covered.

"Of course the first thing we had to do was get our hair fixed. So we all went off to get a permanent wave—and there we were, trying to explain what we wanted in our terrible Portuguese! It was a riot.

"The next thing we did was change the color of our blouses from white to rust, so they didn't show the dirt. Then we changed the skirt from black to some lightweight material in gray. After that we got rid of our hose, because by that time they'd gone into holes and they just couldn't be mended anymore. So we threw them away, and then we moved to divided skirts and finally to slacks—can you imagine?"

"Nobody believed it at first," Gracinha says. "Nuns wearing divided skirts? Whatever next?"

"I guess it must have been a shock to see nuns who didn't wear habits," Joan explains, laughing. "The other thing we did that shocked them, we were the first women to drive. Women did not drive cars. They were entirely dependent on their men. I remember when we wanted an ironing board we went to the sawmill, told them what we wanted, and gave them the measurements. They just looked at us and said, 'Go get your men,' and we said, 'We have no men—this is what we want you to do.' And when they'd made it, we put it on our shoulders and took it down the street to our house. Women didn't do that. We must have broken every rule in the book when it came to what women did or didn't do. We made our own bookcases out of planks stacked up on bricks, and we made the first sink in Coroatá. People used tin basins for washing up and for washing clothes. But the first time we got them to make us a sink, we made one big mistake. Of course there was no drain. So we had them put in a plug—except we told them to put it in the front instead of at the bottom, so the first time we let the water out we all got soaked. I'm sure everyone must have thought we were completely crazy. But we were constantly trying to do little things like that, simple things, to show them that without much you could still live with dignity."

The sisters started by visiting every house in the town to introduce themselves, and then they began to hold impromptu gatherings and Bible study on the street. Their first forays into the countryside were as part of the *desobriga*, regular visits they had to pay to the rural communities, once a month, once a quarter, or, for the outlying areas, once a year. Sometimes they would take the train or a railcar that went along the railroad tracks; sometimes they would climb into the parish jeep and head off as far as the road would take them. When the road ran out there would always be someone on hand with a string of horses or sometimes mules.

Joan remembers that a *desobriga* "was a great occasion, and people used to let off firecrackers as a signal that the *padre* was on his way. So by the time we got there everyone was waiting for us. We'd be given rooms in the landowner's house, there'd be a big feast and mass, and we'd baptize the fifty, seventy-five, or hundred kids who had been born that year and marry everybody who had been living together since last time they'd been visited. The people knew they had to baptize the kids, because they always used to say, 'I want my little creature to be a proper person,' and they knew that if the child died unbaptized, it wouldn't go to heaven. But it didn't take us long to realize that they had no understanding of what it was all about. They'd file into mass in complete silence. It was eerie."

The sisters were troubled by what they saw. "When I realized that the people were just attending mass because they knew they had to, well, it made me cry," says Joan. "They were like cattle being herded, with no idea of what was going on. And the other sisters felt the same. So we sat down together with the priests and we said, 'We have to do better than this. We need to work with the people and see if we can't get some communities up and running.'

"The two priests were great, excellent teachers with lots of good ideas on how to evangelize. They were new to the town and so were we, so we began our ministry together, meeting each evening in our house to talk over what we had been doing, what we had learned, and what we would try to do the next day. Little by little we developed a pastoral plan." A few months after their arrival, the priests went off on vacation to Italy and the sisters took over the religion classes in town.

These were exciting years for the Catholic Church, which had always supported the status quo, the hierarchy, the ruling governments. Before Vatican II, power had been held in the Vatican, by the bishops, and to a lesser extent by the priests. Nuns were considered to have a lesser role, working in education and health and being subordinate to the male hierarchy.

The mass was in Latin, the clergy were the intermediaries between God and the people, and the laity was not encouraged to take an active part in spreading the Gospel. Most Catholic families had a Bible ceremonially placed in their living rooms, where they noted details of family history such as births, marriages, and deaths, but generally their relationship with the Word of God was through the interpretations offered by the parish priest or catechist.

This state of affairs, which had continued virtually unaltered for hundreds of years, was soon to be dramatically changed by the revolution in communications technology. People across the world, now linked by radio and television, began to think of themselves as part of a world community. Cyclones in Bangladesh, earthquakes in China, guerrilla wars in Africa—all these were beginning to intrude on the collective consciousness.

In terms of the Catholic Church, this new thinking led to the formulation of a host of different ways of thinking about the church—in one such avenue of thought the Church was no longer an institution to guide the faithful to salvation but a collection of people, religious and lay, taking a fresh look at the Gospel, following Christ in his option for the poor and the outcasts of society, and working to bring about his kingdom of righteousness and peace here and now. Liberation theology relieved the nuns and priests of the burden of singlehandedly having to bring salvation to the world and immersed the laity in an active participation in church life that had not been seen since the days of the early Christians. None of this would have come about had it not been for the exuberant presence of Pope John XXIII, a man who had a heart for the poor. It was he who charged the church with rethinking its basic tenets and taking its stand with the disadvantaged. It was a challenging responsibility, and the sisters responded joyfully and wholeheartedly.

"It was an incredibly exciting time," Joan remembers. "What came out of all that was that we were to be the church of the poor, which fitted in exactly with what our founder Julie used to say. So we religious used to get together and try to trace out how the church of the poor should operate. We figured out that if we were going to work with the poor, we'd have to live with the poor, live as the poor, and eat like the poor. If manioc flour was all that the people had to offer, that was what we would eat. It took us a while to convince them that we really meant it. And then it was marvelous to see how they started to hold up their heads."

They completely changed the whole idea of church, Gracinha remembers. "Before they came, we used to go to mass because the *padres* told us it was a sin to miss it. But when the young *padres* and the sisters arrived, they turned the whole thing upside down. Suddenly everything came alive in the most amazing way—it was a revelation. Dorothy worked with the adults, Joan worked with the youth, and Bobby led the music. Wonderful music it was, really catchy tunes. And the words were inspiring—they talked about building the Kingdom of Heaven and we really felt that's what we were doing. Dorothy simply loved to sing. One of the songs was about 'Let's go out into the world and get working,' and I chose that song for my wedding because I myself was leaving Coroatá and going out into the world.

"Dorothy used to say, 'Let's go out into the world to the villages.' So we'd make up a little group and take a lantern with us—there wasn't any electricity—and we'd arrive singing these catchy songs and people would come out of their houses and Dorothy would start telling them about the Gospel and we'd have the best time. Those were some of the happiest days of my life."

SIX

GETTING IN DEEPER

"That was how we built the new church," Gracinha remembers. "It was the church of the people, a church where everyone could participate. In the old days the church never used to belong to the poor. It was the church of the rich. Well, the sisters changed all that. They changed the building too, painted it in wonderful bright colors. They kept telling us that the church wasn't the building, it was us, the people of God. Together we built up the base communities and we started youth groups. I remember they told us that we young people were like the yeast in the bread, and it was our job to bring life to the town. We used to put out a little journal. I tell you, it was wild. Nobody ever imagined such a thing!"

Joan takes up the story. "After that first year, we plucked up our courage and we said to the landowners that we weren't going back for the *desobriga* unless the people wanted us there. And we weren't going to stay in the big houses anymore, we wanted to stay with the villagers. Of course the landowners were angry. And the people didn't feel comfortable about having us in their houses, either. They thought they weren't worthy to have the *padre* and the sisters under their roof. They thought we wouldn't be able to eat their food. They were nervous that they didn't have enough. So we said, We'll eat what you eat. If you haven't any food, we won't eat. At first they felt bad, but little by little they realized we meant what we said.

"So there we were, trying to set up base communities all over the place, and let me tell you, we were run off our feet. When we were in the town we felt we ought to be in the rural areas, and when we were there we were worried about who was looking after the town, so in the end we had to divide up the work. I spent my time in the town, and Dot went off into the countryside. And of course the next thing we had to do was get both groups together.

"The priest had a big house, far too big for one person to live in, so we asked him if we could turn it into a parish center, bring in the people from the rural areas and run Bible courses, leadership training, spirituality, and music. Before that, people used to sing those dreary old songs from nineteenth-century Europe, but we started putting words to Brazilian music, and the people simply loved it! Little by little we began to form these communities. We were always looking to find leaders—someone who could read reasonably well and had some leadership qualities."

"Another crazy thing about the sisters was their car," remembers Gracinha. "There was quite a story attached to that car. Seems that before they left America, one of their friends there said, 'Sisters, if I make a lot of money, I'll send you a car.' So they prayed for him, and guess what? He did make a lot of money and he actually sent them a car. It was the only car in town except for the *padre*'s jeep. And there was room in it for lots and lots of people, so they could drive around all over the place. Can you imagine the gossip in the town? Nuns driving a car? Of course it made everything much easier, particularly getting into the backwoods."

But it was still a struggle to communicate, and the Portuguese that the sisters had picked up in the mission training center in Petrópolis still wasn't adequate.

"One day I dropped by their house and there was Joan in floods of tears," says Gracinha. " 'Good heavens, Sister,' I said, 'whatever's the matter?'

" 'Oh, I don't know,' she replied, sniffing. 'I just can't figure out this language. The word for "fork" is masculine and the word for "knife" is feminine and my language doesn't have anything like that and I'm at my wit's end. I'll never be able to speak it properly.' "

"I thought I was just never going to be able to get my tongue around the language," Joan agrees. "I'd be giving instruction to the children and they'd all sit there grinning and I knew perfectly well they weren't understanding a word I said. But Gracinha came up with a solution. She offered to teach us Portuguese, and I said I didn't have the money to pay her and she got quite upset and said she didn't want money and anyway I could help her with her English. So that was the deal. I'd think what I was going to say to the kids, and I'd write it down in Portuguese and then she'd point out my mistakes, and slowly my Portuguese began to improve."

In one of her letters Dot speaks of those early days. "On weekends we used to go off into the countryside and visit the scattered communities. We were on the lookout for lay leaders. Every place we went we concentrated on finding a few people who were willing to get people together, sing, have a Bible reading and reflections. And we'd take one of the *padres* and celebrate mass—always in the homes of these leaders.

"What we'd do is get to the village by the afternoon if we possibly could. We'd organize separate meetings with the youth, the women, and the men, and later on we'd all get together and share our insights. All the groups would have studied the same passage of the Bible, and it was great to hear everyone's views. It was especially good for the women, because when they had community meetings, the only ones who would talk would be the men! And the next day's mass would be based on the reflections of the previous night. So it became a genuine community celebration based on how the people were living and how they were feeling about their lives."

"We started with the men," Joan recalls, "because we knew we could attract the women, no problem. After we had worked with the men, they said to us, 'You know, we know more about religion than our wives and we think you should teach them also.' And they were so proud to be catechists! They wanted to look the part, and they got their wives to make them cassocks so that they looked like priests. We had to laugh, but then we told them tactfully that being a religious leader wasn't about wearing a cassock.

"Little by little we got an educational program up and running. There were no schools in the countryside, but if you could get twenty-five children, you could get money from the government for someone to teach them, and we took great care to try to select teachers who would influence others. And the whole movement just snowballed. By the time we'd been there seven or eight years, the base communities were going great guns and we had a bunch of school groups too. We weren't formally mixed up in politics, but I guess you could say we got involved through the back door, because when you're working to make things better for the poor, you get mixed up in politics without even realizing."

Time passed quickly, what with taking trips to the interior, supervising the schools, giving catechism classes, and getting increasingly involved in the lives of the people. Some of their parishioners found this new participatory way of church too scary, but many of them took to it with considerable enthusiasm and did what they could to create communities where people genuinely cared for each other. Meanwhile the sisters extended their work to prostitutes, young girls from the interior who had few skills and no alternative way to support themselves and their families. They were determined to help these girls find healthier ways of making a living. When asked what they'd really like to do if they had a choice, some of them suggested hairdressing or giving manicures, while others wanted to do dressmaking or crafts. So the sisters organized courses to train them for different professions and placed them in safe houses where they could stay while they were adapting to their new lives. Then they'd move to a neighboring town where nobody knew them, to start afresh.

All of the sisters' work was carried out against the backdrop of an increasingly repressive military government, and the sisters soon got themselves noticed. "It started with our support for rural communities that wanted to build their own schools," says Joan. "Schools were always one of the first things the people wanted. And I remember that many a time the people would build a little school and the landowners would make them tear it down. They didn't want the peasants to learn what was going on in the world. So of course we got into trouble with the landowners. They reckoned we were communists. The people were always in debt to the landowners—I guess you could call it the company store system. They'd sell their crops to the landowner and they'd have to buy their seed from him, and somehow or other the money they made was never enough to cover the money they owed.

"The people were really dirt poor. But it was incredible how they managed to make out. There was always a little manioc flour, a bunch of bananas, a little coffee to drink. They'd have only a few plates and glasses, so we had to take it in turn to eat or have a coffee. But the worst thing wasn't the poverty—it was the fact that they lived in fear. They were afraid of the landowners, afraid of the police, afraid of the army."

"It was a tough time," explains Gracinha. "There were strikes, people getting arrested, the army all over the place. We used to live in fear of the police. But the sisters always told us, 'Don't worry, it'll be all right.' "

Bobby remembers the underlying tension. "By 1968 those of us who were living in Brazil had become aware of the repression and violence promoted by the military dictatorship," she writes. "They had taken over in 1964. It was the time of the Brazilian Miracle, a period of huge economic growth which was later called Savage Capitalism. Everything—the land, the natural resources, the people—was sacrificed in the name of development. Part of the deal was an economic agreement between Brazil and the U.S. favoring multinational companies. The large landowners moved aggressively to buy false titles to state land and to acquire huge tracts of land for agribusiness or as a bargaining chip for some possible future enterprises. People who worked for human rights and for the settlers' rights to the land were labeled subversive, and the government had them hunted down. Military personnel trained at the School of the Americas [the Panama-based training center where Latin American soldiers were taught counterinsurgency techniques] would torture leaders, union members, and those who were working to support them. Death was a price that many paid for envisioning a just society. Everyone who worked for the poor was called a communist. Dot was called a communist. They followed her, photographed her, recorded what she said, and threatened her with imprisonment."

"Oh yes, we were communists, all right," Joan says with a smile. "We were always in trouble with the police. We were followed, watched, accused of providing arms to the peasants—we were accused of everything. Dot was working with the adults, and she just plunged in up to her neck. We used to say, 'Dot, don't do that, you're going to get into trouble.' But she paid no attention. She was really very naive in many ways. She never could understand why the people from different political parties were at daggers drawn during the election campaigns and sitting together drinking beer the day the votes were cast. She simply couldn't get it!

"There was a lot of talk of land reform at the time, and that was something we studied profoundly so we could teach the country people about it. By that stage we had changed our tactics, so that instead of going into the villages for one day, we'd go in for two or three, and we'd do whatever they wanted us to do. We prepared people for marriage, baptism, and the sacraments, but we were also teaching about land reform and citizenship, rights and responsibilities. Explaining that they were people of dignity and didn't have to live like pigs in a sty.

"In one of the little communities, Santo Antonio, the community got together to build a school. A simple little building made of lumber offcuts, but they were proud of it. The next thing that happens, the local landowner sends a truckload of gunmen into the area and makes them tear it down at gunpoint. Not only that, they have to chop the wood into little pieces so they can't use it again. I think the villagers knew that something was in the air, because when they heard the truck coming, they sent their leader off to hide in the forest. The police came along too, arrested a lot of the men and took them off to jail.

"So their wives and children went to the town and we put them all up in the priest's house. The people of Coroatá made sure that there was food and a hammock for everyone. And when the dust had settled, I took the jeep and went back to collect the leader. I bundled him into the car and smuggled him into our garage, and when it got dark we sneaked him into the house. We kept him in the back room for several days, and the police never suspected a thing.

"In the meantime the other guys are still in jail, so Dot and the two priests go over there to see what is going on. This one priest, he's a tall Italian, and he's hanging out around the jail, and the chief of police gets real nervous and tells him to get moving, and the priest says he's not going anywhere until they let those men out because there isn't a reason in the world why they should be in jail. And finally the chief of police loses his cool and says, 'Look here, buddy, if you don't move, you're going to jail too.'

"So the priest says, 'OK,' and he walks right in, and the chief of police throws him into a cell. When Dot sees this, she and the other priest jump into the jeep and head toward São Luis just as fast as they can get that old car to go. By this time it's getting dark, and when the mayor realizes what the police chief just did—because in those days you would never put a priest in jail—he grabs him and drives like a bat out of hell, but Dot is ahead of him, and she gets to São Luis first. It's a long drive, and by the time she arrives it's the early hours of the morning. She goes straight to the bishop and picks him up, and they all go to the head of the military police. By the time the mayor's car gets there, they're all waiting—the bishop, the military police, the civil police, everybody. And they start yelling at the police chief and saying, 'You turn around right now, don't even stop, and you get back to Coroatá and you get that priest out of jail.' So the police chief hightails it back and tells the priest to get out. But *he* gives them the surprise of their lives. Looks them in the eye and says he's not going anywhere without all the others. So they had to let them all out, and the police chief was as mad as a hornet."

As time went by, that sort of incident happened with increasing frequency. "That same police chief tried to throw me in jail once because the kids painted up the walls," says Joan with a big grin on her face. "We had electricity in the evenings from six to ten o'clock, but this one time the mayor had taken the fuel for the town generator to use out on his farm, and the kids had been without classes for two or three months. One night they painted all the buildings with lightbulbs and said, 'We want to study—give us light.' The police chief thought I was responsible for that, which for once I wasn't—so I get this message saying the police are going to throw me in jail since I'm the troublemaker. Well, I say, 'OK, fine. Let me go get my hammock and some books, and you have to promise me you won't let anyone bother me so I can get some rest.' He was so mad he cussed me out and sent me home.

"You need to understand the context," Joan continues. "The military coup had taken place in 1964, before we even got to Brazil. And at first it didn't seem too bad, except that there were lots of police and military about the place. But as time went on, things began bubbling up. Castro had defied the United States, and the politicians had convinced everyone that we were all at the mercy of the Red Peril. So of course the military government in Brazil was always on the lookout for communists. They were terrified that the country would be destabilized by guerrilla incursions, and in the event there were a few isolated guerrilla incidents. The main one was in the neighboring state of Goiás, on the borders of Pará. A long way from Coroatá, but it had the authorities worried. And there were a few communists in Coroatá too, but they weren't guerrillas.

"So when we went around talking about building community and working together, we naturally became the object of great suspicion. Not only were we foreigners, not only did we call ourselves nuns, but we were clearly seditious! A couple of priests were thrown in jail because the police had confiscated some of their song sheets, which said that God created all people equal. That proved they were communists! We had to be on the alert all the time, and sometimes when we'd go into the countryside there'd be a tree across the road, so we always carried a machete or a hatchet. I was working with the youth group, and I'd take the car so we could use the headlights for our meeting. And this strange car would be following me, and sit there with its lights off, and follow me home. They were just trying to intimidate me. We were gone one time and the front of our house was shot up. They knew we weren't there. It was just a message: 'You'd better be careful.' "

At this time the government of Brazil was taking steps to assert its control over the vast empty spaces of the Amazon by encouraging large-scale settlement in the region. The model they chose was based on the settlement of the American West by farmers and cowboys. The farms would be developed by landless migrants from the northeast and the far south, who would settle on the so-called colonization projects, while the ranches would be set up by private individuals, attracted by generous fiscal incentives and the promise of large tracts of land. The occupation of the Amazon was described as a patriotic effort by pioneers, under the slogan "Land Without Men for Men Without Land."

"It was during the early seventies that the government started putting out massive propaganda encouraging people to move into the Amazon and secure the land for the nation," adds Bobby. "Well, as you may suppose, the landless poor saw this as the answer to prayer. They could become homesteaders and actually gain title to their own piece of land. So they came in droves from all over Brazil and started clearing the land and beginning a new life."

To the peasants in Maranhão, it was like a dream come true. They were working as farm laborers, and many of them had migrated from the dry lands in the northeast. So they started packing up their families and heading off into the forest, and later on the sisters decided that one of them should move up there to give the peasants support. Bobby summarizes their feelings: "What was important to us was to care for the people—to help them gain new skills and develop innate talents so they could better cope with their struggles." As the sisters discussed the new situation, Dorothy told Bobby that she thought the community in Coroatá could now fend for itself. She felt that she had given all she had to give, and as she saw more and more people streaming off to try their luck in the new land, her heart called her to pack up and follow them.

SEVEN

LAND WITHOUT MEN FOR MEN WITHOUT LAND

For centuries the inhabitants of the northeastern states had stuck it out in their drought-stricken, dusty land, where the thorn and cactus grew so thickly that the cowboys had to wear leather chaps as they herded their scrawny cattle. They were a mystic people, fiercely independent, faces burned by the pitiless sun, but they loved their land, and despite the years of gnawing hunger they survived, eating dried meat, beans, and manioc flour and waiting for the rain.

It was a land of outlaws, saints, and prophets, and in the early 1900s there arose a prophet called Padre Cícero, of whom the people still speak. He told them that they could escape the great persecution by following the setting sun to the banks of the mighty river and the land of endless green. He told them that they would suffer tribulation, that the river would boil, that there would be a huge battle between the men in green capes and God's people, and that after bitter fighting, good would prevail and the people would live in peace.

And so they started to migrate, a small group here, a small group there, remembering their prophet and answering his call. For weeks on end they journeyed on foot, carrying their bundles, their blankets, and their babies. And when they came to the banks of the Araguaia River and looked across and saw the green forest stretching to the far horizon, they knew that they had found the land of endless green: their promised land.

They crossed the river and settled in the forest, cutting the trees and letting the sunshine in, clearing little plots to plant their manioc, their beans, and their corn, and building primitive houses of wooden saplings with shaggy thatch roofs made from dried grass.

Isolated from the big world, they lived quietly and learned new skills: how to tap rubber and collect Brazil nuts, how to fish, how to hunt in the forest. They learned which plants were good to eat and which served for medicine, and occasionally they would see a riverboat and trade rubber for a little cloth, some shot, a bag of salt. Meanwhile, back in the dry lands, other generations remembered the promises of their prophet, and when the government announced that there was land for the taking in the Amazon region, the people were mindful of Padre Cícero and answered his call.

There were other groups in the forest and along the riverbanks: Indian tribes, descendants of escaped slaves, traders, families who had drifted there over the years and who made a living from hunting and fishing, harvesting the rubber trees that grew scattered in the forest, collecting nuts and forest medicines, the *drogas do sertão*. Some of these families grew rich and acquired the rights to large areas of land, and they built small settlements with churches and schools, where missionary priests and nuns came to work in health and education and teach them about the god of the Christians. These were sleepy little settlements, where the state played little part. There were no lawyers, no judges, and as late as the 1950s, in the town of Conceição do Araguaia, the bishop was considered to be the supreme authority.

But in less than a decade things began to change very rapidly. In the sparkling new capital city, Brasília, built on the high savannas of Goiás, the government was embarking on an extensive program of development aimed at waking the vast lands of Amazônia from their centuries-old sleep. The plan was spearheaded by the construction of two major roads: the Belém-Brasília, linking the new federal capital to the Amazon River, and the Transamazon Highway, which cut through the Amazon forest from east to west and was destined to bring the twin virtues of order and progress to the untamed lands. The government carved the roads out of the red earth, cutting and burning the forest and opening the way for wave upon wave of migrants, who came to set up cattle ranches, to dig beneath the forest floor for gold and minerals, to build towns and factories, railroads and dams. As the new frontier advanced into the forest, people came in the thousands: outlaws and adventurers, pioneers and prostitutes, the poor and the powerful. They came from Minas Gerais, from São Paulo, Espírito Santo, Bahia, from the dry lands of Piauí and Ceará, and from the neighboring states of

Goiás and Maranhão to seek their fortunes in the promised land.

The land-titling system was chaotic, though for centuries it hadn't mattered, since the land seemed endless. Over the years titles had been issued by the counties, the state, and the federal government, and frequently different titles were issued for the same land. There were also different systems of land use, whereby individuals could have a contract with the government to collect rubber or nuts from the Brazil nut or *babaçu* trees. Although the government promised to settle small farmers on the land, the demand far exceeded its ability to do so, and when the new settlers arrived, they found themselves on land that had no title or several conflicting titles, land that was already inhabited, or even land that was claimed by Indians. The shrewder among them figured out the system: all you had to do was go to the notary public and make a land claim, hand over a small sum of money, and the land was yours—regardless of whether or not someone was living on it.

Most people didn't know that they needed to have a piece of paper to prove that they owned the land, so they cleared the forest, planted their subsistence crops, and thought themselves lucky—until the day when a stranger turned up and told them that the land belonged to someone else, that he had the documents to prove it, and that they should pack up their possessions and move on. In such cases, and particularly in view of the fact that the stranger often backed his claim by bringing along a gunman, the wisest course was to pack up and move on. After all, there was always more land.

In Brasília, the government was moving as fast as it could to carry out its ambitious plans for the future of Amazônia. In

1966, two years after the military coup, an agency called SU-
DAM (Amazon Development Agency) was created to speed up
Amazon settlement by financing individuals and corporations,
national and transnational, in setting up large-scale business
ventures, typically sawmills and cattle ranches. The ranches required a large labor force to clear the trees and plant the pastures, and many of the migrants ended up as farm laborers,
sometimes living under a system of debt bondage that was akin
to slavery.

It was in this context of rapid migration, exploitation, and
increasing violence that the Catholic Church set to work, inspired by the spirit of Vatican II, to establish base communities
and form groups for community education. Groups of laypeople
would meet together to study the Gospel in the light of their
everyday experience, trying to relate the teachings of Jesus to
their own reality. Through connecting the Bible stories to their
own struggle, they were encouraged to learn how to read and to
become aware of issues of social justice, such as the right to
clean water, health care, education, and land. It was a way of
bringing them out of their isolation so that they could work together to change their lives.

Meanwhile, a few small groups had quietly arrived in the
forest along the Araguaia River, men and women who had come
from the south with another agenda altogether. They belonged
to the Communist Party, and their aim was to set up a popular
democracy. Fewer than a hundred in number, they worked on
the land, they had skills in health care, and they got along well
with the local people. They also carried out armed training ma-
neuvers under cover of the forest, and for several years their existence passed unnoticed by the authorities. But by 1972 their

cover was blown, and the government dispatched the army posthaste to eliminate them. The soldiers told the villagers that the people of the forests were foreigners, guerrillas, criminals, bank robbers and outlaws, fugitives from justice who were hiding out and plotting to hand over the land to other countries and change the flag from green to red. Many of the villagers who had been discreetly helping the communists went over to the army, trained as forest guides, and helped in hunting down the guerrillas. Others were arrested and beaten up for allegedly collaborating with the enemy. As the skirmishes heated up, the people remembered the words of Padre Cícero and saw the river boil and the military in their green uniforms fighting the people of the forests.

In the last months of 1974, the Sisters of Notre Dame were invited by the bishop of Marabá to come and work in his prelacy, in a small town called Abel Figueiredo, commonly referred to simply as PA 70, after the road on which it was built. On this violent frontier, Dorothy, Sister Becky, and a series of seminarians spent most of their time traveling among isolated settlements. They covered an immense area. Communications were difficult, roads were frequently barely passable, and they were lucky if they made it back to their small house twice or even once a week.

"Dorothy didn't have the patience to stay put once the people had sorted out their problems," says Padre Nello, who remembers her from Coroatá. "She was always looking over to the frontier. There were all those people heading west, and she decided to follow them. Looking for a new land, starting from scratch. They took absolutely nothing. No money, nothing. Building a new life. Dorothy and Becky took themselves off to an area where there wasn't even a *padre*, and they set up the base communities and put everything in place."

Becky takes up the story. "Already while we were in Coroatá, Dorothy was beginning to look west. She was the pioneer type, a real frontierswoman. 'This place is getting too settled,' she'd say. 'I reckon it's time to move on.' But she wanted company, so she invited me to go along. Told me there were Indians in the forest, because she knew how much I wanted to work with them.

"It could hardly have been more different from Maranhão. It was another world. The people there had come from all over—Pará, Espírito Santo, Goiás, Minas—all living together in one little town, all with their different customs and backgrounds, different ways of being Brazilian. We worked with Padre Mário, who used to come out from Marabá, and later he was replaced by Padre Maboni, who came to live in the parish. He was from the south, so he was different too. It was our job to build some sort of community among those groups who didn't trust one another—it was a tough challenge, as you may suppose. It's hardly surprising that some of the sisters didn't think it was a good idea for us to move there.

"But it was a revelation to us, and we simply loved the people. They had such an amazing spirit—they were just determined to make a go of it, and however difficult things were, they never lost hope. They were a tremendous support to us when the going got tough. And it did get tough in all sorts of ways.

"First of all it was the land grabbers. They would wait until the migrants had cleared a little patch of land and then they'd come in and claim it. Threaten people, wave their guns around, burn down the settlers' houses. So we got all the little communities together, documented everything, drew up petitions, and did all we could to publicize the plight of the settlers. As a church we took our stand with the people. We started teaching them about their rights, helping to establish farm workers' unions, giving literacy classes.

"We had a huge area to cover. Our house was halfway down the PA 70. There was nothing there—just a few small towns along the road and some scattered settlements in the interior.

"Of course the people went there to find land. But we quickly realized that there was more to it than that. They'd settle on the land and then there'd be all sorts of trouble. We figured out, Forget it—this isn't about getting the land, it's about staying on it, and we'll have to change our tactics. So in 1976 we set up a training center and we held meetings every weekend. The first week we'd get the men together, then the women, then the youth, and we'd have the fourth weekend free.

"We were working with the Bible—new ways of reading the Bible. People simply loved it. Couldn't get enough of it. We were invited all over in the rural communities to teach literacy, because when people first learn to read, you can't stop them. And the only book they had was the Bible."

By 1975 the army had succeeded in driving the guerrillas from the Araguaia region, but soldiers continued to make sporadic raids in the area of the PA 70. They also remained highly suspicious of those organizations that were working with local communities, in particular the church. Any form of community work was viewed with suspicion and hostility, and repression increased. In July of that year and in response to the deteriorating situation, the National Conference of Bishops set up the Pastoral Lands Commission (CPT), with the objective of supporting the people in their land struggles. Church and community leaders quickly understood the need to work together and began to ally the base communities with the newly established CPT and the educational movement. The military reacted by branding pastoral agents, priests, nuns, and unionists as communists.

"The place was completely under the thumb of the military," explains Becky. "Every time you took the ferry you'd get checked out. Roadblocks everywhere. It was a tough time, and people were armed. No, we never encouraged any kind of armed struggle. We never said you should do that or you shouldn't do that, we just said you should think about the consequences. And then one of the community leaders told us that the people were arming themselves, so we went and told the local colonel that he'd better do something about it. And he did.

"I can never remember a time when it wasn't tense. We were giving a course one weekend when we got a message from the bishop to say that we were wanted in Marabá for questioning by the army first thing next morning. And we had all kinds of papers in the house that you wouldn't want the army to lay hands on. Perfectly innocent stuff, except in that context of paranoia. So we decided that Dot should run on home and take care of it, and she bundled everything up and gave it to one of the neighbors, who buried it in her garden. Just as well, since we later heard that somebody had been through our things, although they didn't ransack the place. At least they left it clean and tidy!

"We went to military headquarters, and I remember that the colonel came out and addressed us in perfect English. He'd learned his trade at the School of the Americas, where the officers were taught about guerrilla warfare—among other things. Dot went in first, and I'm sitting there reading a book and waiting. But when I get nervous I have to go to the bathroom, and they didn't have one for women, so I had to use the men's one, which was all open-plan. Of course I had an escort! And the weird thing was that they kept offering us chocolate . . .

"When it was my turn, they showed me the dossier they had on us. Impeccable. Every paper, every song sheet. I was really impressed! The bishop said to us, 'Whatever they ask you, tell them I told you to do it. Blame it on me.' Well, one of the things they pounced on was the Universal Declaration of Human Rights. We had printed it out and distributed it, and we'd drawn a picture of a big set of scales with a rancher on one side and a bunch of workers on the other. They didn't like that at all, and they wanted to know where we had got the idea from. I had absolutely no idea what I was going to say, but do you know what? We were given the words, just like it says in the Bible. The conversation started out fine, and just when it came to the tough part, the colonel was interrupted by someone and the subject got changed."

As the repression intensified, the sisters became aware that there were others who aligned themselves with the cause. "We used to get the Brazilian news via shortwave radio from Tirana, Albania," Becky adds. "And we knew that there were several groups of people on the same wavelength as us. But we never discovered who they were. The less we knew, the better."

Padre Roberto, a French priest from the prelacy, was arrested and beaten up. His colleagues Padre Humberto and Sister Maria das Graças were accused of being guerrillas. Two other French priests and the Dominican sisters from São Domingos were expelled from the area. Three young lay workers from Rio were arrested and had to be withdrawn. The church in São Geraldo was closed, and some of the parishioners were so frightened that they burned their religious booklets and even their Bibles. Word went out that the sisters were heading up a great movement of subversives, based in Marabá, and fear spread among the communities like wildfire.

A violent conflict exploded in the neighboring parish between a group of settlers and an American rancher who claimed their land. In a climate of increasing tension, thirty settlers were arrested and held without trial, and the parish priest was expelled. Padre Maboni was asked by the bishop to deliver a letter of support to the settlers. The priest was politically conservative and had frequently clashed with Dot and Becky about their political stance, and he was about to transfer out of the prelacy. Yet after a skirmish between the settlers and the police that resulted in several deaths, he was arrested and held for some weeks. Under torture, he alleged that some of his colleagues in the church were subversive, and he was so badly beaten that he was unable to continue working. When the sisters visited him in the hospital where he was recovering, he wept as he told them how badly he had been betrayed by the political system that he had trusted.

In his absence, the sisters found themselves assuming his responsibilities—holding baptisms and weddings, giving communion, anointing the sick and the dying, and providing courage and comfort in the dark days. But worse was to come.

EIGHT

BAPTISM OF FIRE

The rhythm of migration was getting ever more rapid, and in 1977 a new road, PA 150, was opened up to link the main Belém-Brasília highway to the rapidly developing industrial area around Carajás in the south of Pará. Hundreds of settlers continued to pour into the area, and by the following year Dot felt called to move on once again. This time she settled in a community called Arraia (later known as Jacundá), where she worked with Padre Paulinho, Padre Humberto, and a seminarian named Eduardo. Becky stayed on in Abel Figueiredo with another seminarian.

"Dorothy went off to the PA 150 completely on her own," remarks Padre Nello. "Of all the contradictory things to do! It would have been one thing if she'd gone with Becky or with a *padre*, but that's Dorothy for you. Pigheaded. She had her ideas and she wouldn't budge."

"It was the most wonderful area of virgin forest," Becky remembers. "You'd go down the road and be dwarfed by the majesty of the trees. There was nothing there. No settlements. There was one house, which later became Jacundá. The road was unbelievable. Our little Volkswagen Beetle would fall into holes so deep that the men had to pick it up and carry it out. But if you saw it now, you'd weep. The forest has all gone."

"The road was terrible," Padre Paulinho agrees. "There was no power, no health post, no post office, no bank—in fact, there were no public services, no infrastructure of any kind. The migration had begun when the government started work on the PA 150. They hadn't even finished clearing the land before the settlers came streaming in to start their new lives. The vast majority came from the state of Maranhão—forced to leave by the big landowners, people like the Sarney family. They came too from Ceará, Piauí, Pernambuco, and the north of Minas. But it wasn't only the settlers. Others started arriving, from Minas, Espírito Santo, and Bahia, and that group came for a different reason—they wanted to lay hands on large areas of land. Some of the more powerful managed to get financing from SUDAM, but most of them arrived with a little money that they had received from the sale of their land back in their home states. The poor, of course, arrived with nothing.

"Neither the government nor private companies had ever set up any colonization projects in that area, and the only settlers were those who came of their own accord. The government agencies arrived later, to try to sort out the land titling, which was in a state of total confusion. The big guys got their way by the simple expedient of bribing the land officials, grabbing more and more land, and calling in the police to evict the settlers. These evictions were extremely violent—houses and fields were burned, and the men were arrested, tortured, and thrown into jail.

"The 'parish' was enormous. We used to get around as best we could on public transport, trucks, horses, bikes, and usually on our feet. We never had any kind of vehicle. The prelacy of Marabá was always supportive, especially the bishop, Dom Alano.

"Dorothy's main focus was on education," Padre Paulinho continues. "There were virtually no schools, and most of the adults were illiterate. She went all out, setting up meetings to discuss who was interested in becoming a teacher, taking the list of names to the mayor, and doing what she could to get hold of textbooks. The teachers usually hadn't studied beyond the fourth grade themselves. It was the settlers who built the schools, simple little constructions made of saplings with straw roofs. To them, the important thing was to have a school where their children could learn to read and write. Those were heroic days—people really pulled together. There was very little in the way of equipment, and the teachers were paid practically nothing, when they were paid at all."

Marga, the ombudsman from Belém, describes a visit that she paid to Dorothy in Jacundá. "She was living in a beat-up wooden building belonging to the farm workers' union. Two rooms, and the roof leaking like a sieve. Dorothy had all her things piled up on a shelf covered with plastic—papers, files, boxes of documents, a couple of changes of clothes. And there wasn't a morsel of food in the house. I looked in the kitchen and all I could find was half a dozen cans, the ones you use for storing rice and beans. Well, they were all empty except one, and that had a bare handful of manioc flour.

"One of the settlers, Zé Pião, had been killed and we'd gone there to show our support. We arrived there covered in dust, took a shower, hung our hammocks—I remember we had to move them several times on account of the leaking roof—and made some tea. Then Dorothy sent us all to different houses to get something to eat. Simple food—rice and beans, squash and a bit of dried meat. The families shared what little they had. That's solidarity for you.

"The next day we left early. It had been raining and there was mud everywhere. One of the planks was missing in the flatbed of the truck and the mud came splashing through. We did what we could for the family of Zé Pião, and then we headed back to town. By the time we got there it was three o' clock and we were all starving. We got down off the truck and had a confab. What on earth were we to do? There wasn't a thing to eat in the house. The market was just closing, but fortunately we managed to find a little manioc and some meat. We took it home and cooked it and then we called Dorothy and said, 'Let's eat.' And she dug into that food and started laughing. Told us she couldn't remember the last time she'd eaten meat. She'd forgotten what it tasted like.

"Next day we held a service in the church, and some of the ranchers who were mixed up in the death of Zé Pião were there. So Dot goes up to them and starts talking about it, and they tell her straight out that the church isn't the place to talk about things like that. One of our group weighs in and tells them that the Bible is always talking about justice. Rolling like a river, that's what he said. The ranchers didn't like that at all.

"Dorothy refused to let one of those ranchers be godfather to one of the children. Told him he wasn't behaving in a Christian way. So of course she began to make enemies. But she was dearly loved in the community, especially among the poor. She'd walk down the street and everyone would run up to talk to her."

Padre Roberto was working in the same area. "Oh yes, I knew Dorothy," he says. "We never worked in the same parish, but I was in the same prelacy. She went to Abel Figueiredo in 1974, and five years later she moved to Jacundá and got mixed up with the land conflicts. It was a very violent area, and there were a lot of conflicts. One time they issued a warrant for her arrest, but luckily she was tipped off in time to get out. They dropped the matter, but they warned her that if she continued to meddle in the land issue, she'd find herself in deep trouble.

"It was a tough job trying to create a community spirit," he continues. "We were looking for ways to link people together—base communities, community associations, Farmers' Days—the sorts of things that could help them build their lives, their struggles and their dreams. For the settlers it was something completely new, and they loved it, because they felt supported. They could go to Dorothy's house or to Paulinho's house and know they'd be safe. Sometimes they'd hide out there when the going got tough. But the ones who hated it were the ranchers. Some of them would stop at nothing. They used to have people eliminated. And the settlers carried guns as well. It was an armed conflict. A war, really.

"We ourselves were never in favor of violence. Our job was to help the settlers organize themselves into communities and join the unions so they could fight for justice, roads, schools, and their rights. But always through nonviolent means. Yes, a lot of communities were set up, but all too often the people lost heart, and with good reason—there was just no way they could hold out on the land. No roads, no chance of selling their crops, no health care—malaria was especially bad—and a total lack of any government policy to support them. Many of them simply sold up and moved to the city, went back where they came from, or took their chances in the goldmines.

"The army had arrived in Marabá during the 1970s, to help build the Transamazon Highway and particularly to fight the guerrillas. We knew that we were being watched, but they never interfered with us directly. But the military police, that was another thing altogether. They were always visible, always violent toward the settlers over the question of the land. We were threatened, slandered in the press, and accused of instigating land invasions. I was arrested and beaten up so badly I had to leave the area for a few months until things cooled down, and Sister Dorothy had to do the same.

"We always knew there were death lists," says Padre Paulinho. "They were even published in the national press. Some of the people on those lists were eliminated—Paulo Fontelles, João Batista, Gringo, Gabriel Pimenta. And our names were on the list too."

"Padre Paulinho used to receive death threats," says Padre Roberto. "They set up an ambush to catch him once, but he got away and went off to São Paulo to let things cool down. I celebrated Christmas mass in his place, and I took the CPT Toyota. On the way back there was a tree across the road, and I could see gunmen off in the forest. But I was OK. They weren't after me. Those were perilous times, but the *padres* had to face them, right? And there was Dorothy, going out to meetings with the farmers and helping them get organized. Sometimes I had to calm her down because she'd say too much. She'd encourage them to resist at all costs. I used to say, 'Calm down, Dorothy, people might get you wrong, don't you see?' She was very—well . . .

"The place was crawling with police. The army was stationed in Marabá, closer to the area where they'd had the guerrillas. Police all over the place, watching, watching. Bad people. Terrible. Lots of conflict, lots of people getting killed. There was a massacre in Goianésia—they killed a child. There were these gunmen surrounding the settlers, and this old man comes along carrying a child, and they shot the old man and killed the child too. The old man and the child dropped dead at the same instant. They just came along, stuck the gun to the old man's head, and blasted it right off.

"If you were working in that area, it was a question of kill or be killed. These days the frontier has moved on, but wherever you get new areas being opened up, that's what happens. On one side you get the big guys, speculators, who want the land so they can sell it on, and on the other you get the little guys, who want the land so they can make a living. That's all they want to do—simply find a way to stay alive. It's a permanent state of conflict.

"So there's Dorothy, in the 1970s, face-to-face with this situation. She'd taken her stand with the poor and she knew the risks. The people weren't organized—they'd come from all over, and nobody trusted anybody. But they did trust the church—it was the focus of resistance. Between them they organized Farmers' Day on July twenty-fifth. It was a big feast day, lots of banners, beautiful to see. The power of the people, people working together to win a piece of land. Working together with each other, with the church, and with the union.

"Is the land fertile? Well, no. Our soil isn't very good. They'll plant grass, and after a couple of years it'll turn yellow. There's a layer of topsoil, but underneath it's all sand. And when they cut the forest there's nothing but sand, great sandy patches in the pastures. In those days all they did was slash and burn. So the settlers could never really make ends meet. They'd clear the undergrowth, cut the forest, burn it, make a little clearing, burn it again, and then plant. If you have a big area, maybe 250 acres, you can make out. You can plant your rice and beans. But if you cultivate the same area year after year, all you'll get is sand. Unless you use a lot of fertilizer, and small farmers haven't got the money for that.

"Did the place get tamed over the years? Well, maybe. But it's not good now either, because the settlers moved in, but then they started selling up. At the end of the day, what you have in that area is big ranches. The settlers left because there was no support for them. With slash and burn there's no structure, no stability, no respect for the forest. That type of agriculture isn't sustainable. But it's all they know. And when the soils wear out, all they know is how to plant pasture. But there's no way they can raise cattle. They need fences and they can't afford them, so they sell up and move on. This business of land reform—it may keep them alive, but there's no future in it. The government isn't interested in small farmers. All it cares about is soy, timber, cattle ranching. Nobody cares about the small farmers. Nobody. Except the landless movement."

As Dorothy got more and more involved, it became increasingly clear both to her and to her colleagues that if she didn't mind her step, she was going to find herself in serious trouble. She had also noticed, with growing concern, that between them, the settlers, large and small, had succeeded in destroying the forest and destroying their own livelihoods. There had to be a better way. So in 1982, with the blessing of the bishop of Marabá, she traveled the Transamazon Highway to the river town of Altamira, presented herself to the bishop, Dom Erwin, and told him she wanted to work with the poorest of the poor. She was fifty-one years old, and before she left, she confided in Becky that although she was a nomad at heart, she felt that this would be her final move.

NINE

THE TRANSAMAZON HIGHWAY

On a hot, humid October day in 1970, the president of Brazil, General Médici, and his delegation arrived in Altamira to mark the beginning of a glorious future: integrating Amazônia with the rest of Brazil through the construction of the 1,800-mile Transamazon Highway, also known as the Transamazônica. With the motto *Amazônia é nossa* (Amazônia is ours), the highway was designed to integrate the huge forgotten region with the rest of Brazil, bringing order and progress, industry and agriculture, and making available the land without men for the men without land. All at the expense of the existing scattered populations of Indians, river people, rubber tappers, goldminers, and pioneer settlers.

The Brazilian press gave fulsome praise to this momentous occasion. "General Médici presided yesterday in the county of Altamira in the state of Pará over the opening ceremony of the great Transamazon Highway," proclaimed the *Folha de São Paulo*, "which is destined to cut across the whole of Amazônia from east to west, a distance of more than 1,800 miles, linking this region to the northeast. The president, deeply moved, watched while a tree measuring 150 feet was felled along the line of the future highway, and then unveiled a commemorative plaque affixed to the trunk of this huge tree on which were written the following words: 'Here, on the banks of the Xingu River, in the heart of the Amazon jungle, the President of the Republic commemorated the first step in the building of the Transamazon Highway, a historic advance in the conquest of this giant green forest.' "

Two years later the president returned to inaugurate the first stretch of highway. "Returning to the historic banks of the River Xingu where he had overseen the first steps in the construction of the immense highway that will unite the country, President Emílio Garrastuzu Médici today opened the first stretch of the Transamazônica between the rivers Tocantins and Tapajós, embodying the determination of the Brazilian people to construct a great and vigorous nation."

The objective was to people the region by relocating surplus populations from the far south and the drought-stricken northeast, to attract investment and create infrastructure, and to prove to the world that both Amazônia and its immense mineral, biological, and hydrological resources were in the hands of Brazil and not up for grabs by the international community.

In the distant offices of Brasília, planners marked out a

straight line linking Altamira with Itaituba to the west, and traced in a series of smaller roads—known as *travessões*, or transversal roads—to give access to the land in the interior. Five hundred families were settled on 250-acre lots, settlements with schools, health posts, and trading posts were built, and while waiting for their first harvest, each family received a minimum salary per month (around US$60). They were encouraged to plant subsistence crops (rice, beans, and corn) as well as bananas, sugar cane, fruit trees, coffee, and cocoa. The project looked very nice on paper, but in practice the tropical soils were easily exhausted, the roads became impassable in the rains, the settlers had no way of selling their surplus, and when, in the mid-1980s, government credits for smallholders were discontinued, many of them simply gave up and moved away.

Despite extravagant claims made by the government, the lack of supervision was such that barely ten years later, in 1982, the Pará state secretary for public security sent a message to the Ministry of Justice describing the land situation as totally uncontrolled. He spoke of land invasions on all sides; wholesale theft of timber; groups of desperately poor settlers with access to neither roads, schools, nor health care; indigenous lands with no demarcation; a police force that was completely underequipped; and a legal system that was unable to function.

The lands on the Transamazon East, the road from Altamira to Marabá, were designed not for smallholder colonization but for large landholdings of 7,500 acres. Government contracts granted ownership of the land after five years if agricultural or ranching projects had been established. Failure to do so meant that the land reverted to the federal government, but in practice this was never enforced, and the steady trickle of newcomers continued to brave mud and malaria to settle wherever they could, frequently on land that had been licensed to absentee landlords. In 1995 new lines of smallholder credit were opened, and the rate of migration increased as people poured into the area once again.

As the migrants trekked onto the *travessões*, many of the original concession-holders suddenly remembered their long-abandoned claims to the backlands and, scenting the possibility of greatly increased land values, made plans to reoccupy the land, extract the timber, and set up the ranches that had been projected twenty years earlier.

For decades the land wars had followed the advance of the agricultural frontier as it moved west into the virgin lands of the Amazon. The first area of conflict, in the 1960s, had been around Paragominas, on the Belém-Brasília highway, due south of Belém. By the 1970s the conflicts had moved west to the PA 150 around Jacundá, where Dorothy was working. A decade later the focus was in the south of Pará, between Marabá and Santana; in the 1990s, southwest to São Felix do Xingu; and in the early years of the new century, due west along the Trans-amazônica, into the Terra do Meio, between the Xingu and Tapajós rivers and down the BR 163, which links Santarém to Cuiabá in Mato Grosso. Once again Dorothy was to find herself in the eye of the storm as she moved into that area and started to work with the landless settlers on the Transamazônica.

Dom Erwin, bishop of the Xingu, takes up Dorothy's story. A native of Austria, he succeeded his uncle, the previous bishop, in the mid-1960s. He knows his huge prelacy extremely well, is a doughty champion of human rights, and speaks flawless Por-tuguese.

"What an extraordinary woman Dorothy was," he says. "One of many in these parts. And believe me, I know the Xingu region like the back of my hand. Been here for forty years, and I've been bishop for twenty-five. I could write a book about the women of the Xingu. And one of them would be Dorothy.

"I don't deny that she was a bit of a Samaritan, but deep down she was more of a prophet. Prophets are those who tell forth the will of God—God's deepest desire. The prophet doesn't have a voice of her own. The prophet is the spokeswoman. She speaks for God. She feels this as her mission, feels called to do this. So when we think of Dorothy, this is the starting point.

"I met Dorothy in 1982. She arrived in Altamira alone. Told me she'd come from Marabá. I gathered there had been some problem there, something connected to the land. I never found out what it was. She'd been working with the settlers and the landowners didn't like her. I don't know if the church backed her—I never checked it out, never asked the bishop or anyone. She didn't tell me and I didn't ask.

"She turns up in Altamira. Tells me her name is Dorothy Stang, she's an American from Ohio, a sister of Notre Dame de Namur, and she wants to work in the Xingu among the poorest of the poor. Wants to give her life for people living in abject poverty. So I said, 'All right, Dorothy, if you're looking for the poorest of the poor, you'll need to go to the Transamazon East. It's the end of the world there. It's terrible. The people haven't got so much as a place to lay their bones.' Well, she agreed, and off she went.

"I had my doubts, I can tell you. Not about her as a person, but about the manner of her coming. Generally speaking, it's not the nun herself who says where she wants to go. Normally it's the congregation that gets in touch, and there are all sorts of bureaucratic procedures to go through. Well, nothing like that ever happened. They never wrote to me, and I never contacted them.

"She started work at kilometer 96, a place called Nazaré. She lived in a mud house belonging to one of the settlers. Once in a while there'd be someone working with her, but there was no formal agreement—they never set up a convent or anything. She was always pretty independent, never much of a one for working in a team. She *was* the team! She had her own ideas, her own vision, and she got on with it. Sometimes I'd say to her, 'Look here, Dorothy, I'd like you to work more closely with your colleagues, just be a little bit more collaborative.' And she'd always promise that she would. It wasn't that she was opposed to it, she just couldn't do it. It wasn't her style.

"Lots of families were moving in at the time. They came from all over the country, and she felt that her job was to get them to work together to the point that they could set up associations and cooperatives and so on. She even managed to get a truck for them, but that didn't work! She never charged anything—everyone wanted to use it, but nobody wanted to pay. So of course it came to nothing.

"The people worshipped her. If any decision had to be taken, they'd always say, 'Let's ask Sister Dorothy.' It was like she was the Queen Mother, savior of the nation. She got jobs for people, she helped them over the land issue. She set up a fruit processing factory. And she worked hard for the women. They were considered inferior. And if they were black or Indian, worse still. She really had compassion for them—she helped them realize their worth. That was one of the great things that she did in Nazaré.

"It's funny, really—people talk as if she was a saint. She was no saint. She could be very difficult, you know. Stubborn as a mule. Once she made up her mind, she wouldn't budge an inch. Not that I wasted my breath arguing with her. If she was being particularly pigheaded, I'd say, 'For heaven's sake, Dorothy, have a little sense!'

"But do you know something? She never lost her smile. She just went ahead, did what she thought was right, and never wavered. They never ground her down. I never had any problems with her myself. She used to stay in my house, and in the later days she had the room next to mine. She was a member of the family—she used to come and go when she wanted, she knew where things lived, she ate with us, although she preferred to eat in the kitchen. She'd go upstairs, use the living room, use the phone. Sometimes she'd make a favorite dish of hers, and I thought that was great.

"In terms of the prelacy, she wasn't a loose cannon, although there were people who thought she was. She valued our work, always turned up at our meetings, took part in prelacy affairs with great enthusiasm. If I asked her to do something or join some commission, she never refused. If she hadn't been murdered, nobody could have taken her from the Xingu. I was convinced she'd stay here till she died. But I never expected her death to be the way it was.

"She was becoming well known, not only on the Transamazônica. She was widely loved. But she was hated too. People on the street used to speak badly of her. Malicious gossip, even on the television. Sometimes I had to speak up for her, and I used to say, 'Look, if you're accusing Dorothy of something, I'd like to see proof.' They accused her of arming the peasants, and I'd say, 'This is absurd. She doesn't even know which way to hold a rifle, much less a revolver.' I told them, 'Look, she may have her shortcomings, as we all do, but she'd never, ever do such a thing.'

"She just couldn't accept the way that the poor were living, and she did what she could to change things. She'd go to Belém, and if she couldn't get things sorted out there, she'd be in Brasília before you could turn around! There was no holding her. In fact, she got what she wanted, as often as not. With the federal police, for example, and the federal attorney's office. And she started getting recognition.

"I was there in the legislative assembly when she got that award—honorary citizen of the state, I think it was. She wasn't too happy about it, because others were being honored and she didn't want to appear in the same photograph with some of those people who wouldn't normally speak to her. It put her squarely in the public eye, and there were those among the politicians who figured she was some sort of foreign nun hiding out in Anapu and working against them.

"I'm not sure if she really understood politics. She knew who she was talking to, and she told it like it was. She didn't invent and she didn't exaggerate. She stuck to the facts and gave her interpretation. And most people thought it was great.

"She was an attractive woman, you know. Not beautiful, but she had a winning way. A very gentle manner. She spoke softly. Her voice was so soothing that sometimes I'd be listening to her and I'd have to pinch myself to stay awake. She had an easy way with her, very relaxed. She'd come into the house, sit down in the kitchen, ask questions, tell jokes, smile. Chatting away in that broken Portuguese of hers—all her life she used to mix up masculine and feminine. It was a standing joke. She never did learn to speak the language properly.

"She treated everyone alike. Called them by name, whoever they were. And that was her downfall. She told everyone who the land grabbers were, where they lived. And of course they hated her for it. I heard them say so. They used to talk to me, and I said to them, 'Listen here. If you are the legitimate owners of the land you occupy, you'll need to prove it. Show me the land title. The real thing, not some faked document. And if you can prove you are the legitimate owners of the land, I'll be the first to defend you. I won't go against the evidence, against the law or the constitution. I'm not against the rule of law. This country lives by the rule of law, and as a citizen it's my duty to defend the federal constitution.' But I've seen no proof to this day. And Dorothy is dead.

"These accusations against her—it wasn't just once. There's a mafia of people around here who do things in the dark, quietly, in the dead of night. I can't prove it, but everyone says that the ranchers had a meeting in a hotel in Altamira at the beginning of 2005 to plot Dorothy's murder. And when the word gets out on the street, people exaggerate, but they don't invent. Nobody has ever investigated this meeting to find out who was there plotting in the dead of night.

"So what was this sustainable project all about? I see it as an attempt, a very modest one, by the government to do a new kind of land reform on the Transamazônica. The people for whom Dorothy was fighting, they were her people and she was theirs. Not that she was their boss, but they considered her to be their big sister. She was a matriarch. I always used to laugh be-cause she always called them 'my people.' She identified with them, body and soul. These sustainable projects of hers, they were an important step. But they were a slap in the face to the rich and greedy—that's why they went after her. She never gave in—she was sure that the government would support her. You could say she was a martyr for land reform, because she fought tooth and nail for what the government wanted. And now that they've finally got going, she's gone."

Brother Jerônimo vividly remembers those early days. "I met her in 1982," he says, "during a diocesan assembly on the Xingu. I'd heard talk of this American woman who went around the back roads on a scooter. When it was raining hard or she couldn't get through, she'd leave her scooter in the nearest house and head off on foot. She rarely traveled by bus, because she didn't have the fare. If she wanted to go longer distances, she'd hitch a ride on top of a truck. She once hitched 900 miles on a truck. Wherever the poor needed help, she'd be there. She drew her strength from the Bible and the Book of Hours. On her travels she'd make a point of sleeping in the wayside chapels, simple shelters made of saplings with grass roofs. She counseled the farmers, lived with them, ate what little they had to offer but was always sensitive to their lack of resources. She used to set up meetings, help them to work together, demarcate their land, and get their title. By law they were entitled to a 250-acre lot within thirty miles of the highway, 600 acres if they lived farther away.

"But even then she used to receive death threats from the land grabbers and the ranchers in the region. I remember once when she was working with the settlers to stop their trees be-ing cut, there was an ambush, and they only survived because they took shelter behind a truck. In those days Pacajá and Anapu were known for harboring outlaws and fugitives from Marabá, from Tocantins or Maranhão. They used to make the settlers' lives a living hell. The Transamazon East was more sparsely inhabited than the western section—the soils were poor, and the area was plagued by malaria, particularly cerebral malaria. The government health agency simply couldn't keep up, and the people used to spend what little they had on medicine or traveling to the hospital in Altamira. Not many people would agree to work in the area, and Dorothy used to get malaria all the time.

"My work consisted of setting up schools and training teachers throughout the whole 180,000 square miles of the prelacy. We managed to raise the money to build a couple of teacher training centers, and Dorothy took it upon herself to help identify candidates. She quickly perceived the difficulty for the students in traveling great distances and staying away from their families for prolonged periods of time. They couldn't take it, and the dropout rate was high, so she insisted that we open another training center for the Transamazon East, serving the area from Anapu to Pacajá. In that way the teachers could visit their families more regularly, and that kept them going.

"She got the families together and invited one of her nephews from America to come lend a hand. He was an engineer and offered to help build the training center. They built it from mud and straw and saplings and called it the Centro de Nazaré, which means the Nazareth Center.

"So in 1984, before the building was completed, we started the first training course, with forty-one women and nine men, most of whom had been selected by Sister Dorothy. The course was held in two modules, one in January and February and the other in July. During the rest of the year the buildings were used for leadership training, union meetings, retreats, and farmers' meetings. I used to spend a lot of my time traveling along the Transamazônica supervising the courses, and many an evening Dorothy and I would sit together talking about a thousand things, from environmental protection to sustainable development, health, and whatever ways we could think of making people's lives better."

Two of Dorothy's friends from the interior share their memories of those early days. "Dorothy came here in 1983," says Isa, one of the local community leaders, a strong woman with a forthright manner. "The government had just dumped us on the Transamazônica, like a herd of cattle. We were left to get on with it. There was no school, no nothing. The government wasn't interested in the little people. Dorothy came and began to work with the community, starting in Nazaré. She encouraged us to work together, and she managed to get us a teacher training course. There was only one school, just the first few grades. Later on she went to Belém and told them we needed a high school. And we set up schools in the interior. I remember we teachers once went six months without being paid. But we didn't give up. And it was Dorothy who used to go to Belém and get our money.

"And then we started fighting for the land. This section of the Transamazônica wasn't designed for small farmers. It was meant for ranching. Well, we went around setting up base communities and talking about our needs. We established the Pioneer Association and started demanding everything—land, roads, school, health posts. And then we set up the Women's Association.

"We opened some little stores, and with the profit we made we set up more. We started with two chickens, and then we bought pigs and finally a heifer. In those days it was really difficult to get to Altamira. The roads were terrible. So we sold cooking oil, a bit of rice, and then we opened a warehouse, so that people didn't need to go to Altamira for stores. We had a truck that brought supplies for resale. The idea wasn't to make a profit—we invested the money back in the warehouse. It lasted for a couple of years, but then there was inflation and we lost control. So we decided to sell out and start a fruit processing plant.

"It was all thanks to Sister Dorothy. She fought for us tooth and nail—went on a hunger strike, slept on the sidewalk in Brasília, never gave up. If it hadn't been for her, we'd have nothing here. She was always looking out for us. And what she left us was the heritage of knowing how to work together and share things."

Rosária agrees, her green eyes sparkling. "Dorothy was a shining light for us. When we arrived on the Transamazônica, it was the end of the world. We were abandoned by the church, by the state, by everyone. And Dorothy was like a light to us. We realized that it was possible after all to live in Amazônia. We started working together. We learned to love the forest. We saw that we women had to take up the challenge, and we founded the Women's Association. The men used to be very macho, so we started going to meetings and talking about health, politics, education, alternative medicine. We only had seven schools, and we managed to set up another twenty-three! We got together to build the schools, and Dorothy found the teachers.

"And we fought for the land, started thinking about farming the land more sustainably. The families kept coming in, and we kept organizing ourselves. Today I can feel her presence among us very strongly. We are working right now just as she used to work. Lots of young people are joining the struggle—Dorothy's disciples.

"There are still all sorts of problems—fights over the land, over the roads. But I'm very hopeful that things will get better. We're getting stronger all the time."

TEN

LIFE ON THE TRANSAMAZÔNICA

From 1978 to 1985, Padre Lucas was the priest in charge of the remote communities scattered along the Transamazônica East. One month he would visit the distant settlements in the interior, and the next month he would bring some of the people into the tiny settlement of Centro de Nazaré, which he founded in 1980. "It consisted of a dormitory, a meeting place, and a small house which later became the sisters' house. We built everything out of wood, sawn by hand, and the only thing we had to buy were the nails," he remembers. Travel was grindingly difficult—the roads were dusty in the dry season and covered in glutinous mud during the rains—but he persevered, and in 1982 he was joined by Sister

Dorothy. "It was the Wild West in those days," he says, laughing. "Lots of conflict, lots of deaths. I used to work with the Franciscan sisters, and we considered ourselves missionaries, setting up the base communities. We didn't get involved in the land struggles until Dorothy came. She opened our eyes to the problem."

When Dorothy arrived in Nazaré in 1982, the huge county of Senador Porfírio consisted of 4,600 square miles, five times the size of Rhode Island. Its population was around 8,000. She had asked to work with the poorest of the poor, and her wish had been granted. And she had no illusions about the task at hand. "We can't *talk* about the poor," she wrote. "We must be poor with the poor, and then there is no doubt how to act."

The first thing she did was to get together with the people so they could figure out what they needed most. "There was no infrastructure at all," says Geraldo, a son of one of the settler families, who later became an agricultural technician and worked closely with Dorothy. "Absolutely nothing. The truth was that the area had never been designed for small farmers—it was set up for logging and ranching. So there were no schools, no health posts, no government assistance of any kind."

In those days Maria dos Santos (later to become Sister Maria) lived with her family at the very end of one of the back roads that transect the Transamazônica like fish spines. "The first time Dorothy came to our house we all ran and hid," she recalls with a laugh. "My father was convinced she must have come to take our land away. We didn't have any title or anything like that. But then she said she wanted to set up a base community and asked if we'd be willing to help. So we started talking about what we needed, and of course the first thing that everybody wanted was a school."

The Centro de Nazaré was two hundred miles west of the violent south of Pará where Dorothy had previously been working, but the situation there was no less precarious. The settlers who were swarming into the region from all across the country had become deeply suspicious, not only of the government but also of each other. They needed to work together and to learn to trust one another. They had no land and few skills except their courage and the strength of their arms. So they became builders, and over the space of twenty-four years they built more than fifty schools.

Their plan was to strengthen their community by any means they could, so that they could claim and keep the land and make it productive. In 1983 the pastoral team was reinforced by the arrival of Sister Rita, and in July of that year the community celebrated its first Farmers' Day, later to become the high point of the year. People streamed in from the distant settlements, bringing sacks of rice and beans, and each group presented itself, told its story, and celebrated its history. Festivals, Bible courses, and farmers' meetings provided a rare chance for people to get together, exchange news, laugh, and relax, with volleyball for the young, games for the kids, and food that was prepared and eaten together.

The first school they built was in a community called Pau Furado (Broken Tree), and no sooner was it completed than every little community wanted one. But where were they to find the teachers? They would have to come from the local communities, where there was unlikely to be anyone with even a fourth-grade education. Those teachers would need to be trained and they would need a training center. As if in answer to a prayer, Dot's nephew Richard promised to help out, and when he arrived from the States in November 1983, Dot put him in charge of building the nucleus of the future training center: classroom, dormitories, kitchen, and chapel. A faded photograph dated December 1983 shows Dot proudly nailing up a sign saying CENTRO DE NAZARÉ TRAINING CENTER. Two months later, with the bare bones of the center in place, the first teachers arrived to begin their course.

Early photographs, many of them severely damaged by humidity and termites, chronicle the founding of the Associação Pioneira, or Pioneer Association. Its early activities included religious instruction, education, and the purchase of the first rice-hulling machine, since cleaned rice commanded a higher price. Photographs of Dot show her posing under a banner saying AS-SOCIAÇÃO PIONEIRA TRANSAMAZÔNICA, handing out small blackboards, supervising a first communion where all the children are dressed in white, and dancing the *forró* with a big grin on her face. Other photographs show a group of women with a banner saying WOMEN UNITED IN CONTROL OF OUR FUTURE; families posed in groups or lounging in hammocks; the first classroom; Bible study in the sisters' house; a truck sporting a banner for land reform; Dot in an Amazônia T-shirt; and people making baskets, painting murals, digging wells, and plastering houses.

Nineteen eighty-four was a year of solid achievement. The sisters gave their first catechism course, a second rice-hulling machine was installed, and discussions were held about opening a community trading post. Padre Lucas twinkles as he recounts the story. "The first thing that happened was that Dorothy held a meeting with eight women to sell them the idea. They loved it! 'It's a great idea,' they said. 'But what are we going to use for capital?' So she went home and she thought and she thought, and at the next meeting she said, 'Does everyone here keep chickens?' And they said, 'Of course!' So she said, 'OK, next week I want each of you to bring your best chicken.' And they sold them and bought a pig. It was the skinniest pig you ever saw, but they arranged to send it to live in every household, one after another, for a month. It grew extremely fat, and then they bred it and it had nine piglets, and that's how they raised the money to get started. I just wanted to tell you that to show you how amazingly creative Dorothy was!"

In April 1984, Dot returned to the States to visit her ailing mother, who was being cared for by her brother David. Edna was eighty-five years old, and Henry was eighty-seven, and this was to be the last time that Dorothy saw her mother.

The following year she had a visit from two of her sisters, Mary and Maggie. There was much to show them: the coffee bushes that had been planted along the riverbanks to provide enough coffee for everyone; the minitractor that they had ac-quired thanks to a donation; the improvements to their house (an extra room, plastered walls, and a wood shingle roof). There were stories to tell around the table in the evenings: how the Transamazônica was impassable for months on end, forcing peo-ple to travel to Belém by river, and how they decided to barri-cade the bridge over the Anapu River and stuck it out for three weeks, until the authorities were finally forced to fix the road. There were tales of simmering land disputes; the visit from staff of the land reform agency INCRA, who had been lodged in the men's dormitory; the day they had planted trees around the church; the donation they had received to help them set up stores in the rural areas. And always plans—plans to build more schools, to get the women working together, to figure out how

to get some form of transport so the settlers could sell their surplus in town, to train agricultural technicians within the community, to find ways of generating more income, to improve family health, and most of all to help people take responsibility for their lives.

Over the years these dreams were realized, little by little. The buildings got upgraded, and mud floors were replaced by cement. The first group of teachers graduated and went to work in the rural areas. The Women's Association was founded, focusing on family health, alternative medicine, and better diet, and the first Women's Assembly was held. A companion diocese in California raised the money for a truck and donated it to the Pioneer Association. Lovingly known as Amarelão (Big Yellow), the truck was blessed by the *padre* and sent to work. For five years it never missed its weekly trip to Altamira, carrying produce and people and buying supplies for the community store.

"There was only one bus in those days," remembers Giovanni, Geraldo's brother. "Transbrasiliana was the name of the company. It still runs. But in those days they used to charge five days' wages just to get to Altamira."

"And it only went along the main highway," confirms Geraldo. "It never went on the back roads. You could wait three days for it to come, and that was in the dry season. During the rains it didn't come at all, and people used to spend months without being able to get out."

"When we got the truck, we broke the monopoly," adds Giovanni. "Other people started up with alternative transport, and now instead of charging five days' wages, the bus company charges one."

By 1989 things were progressing steadily. Dot took a trip to California to thank the diocese of Paraíso for their gifts of money. She was unanimously selected by the Justice and Peace Committee of Springfield, Ohio, as the missionary they would support, and she received a visit from the mission coordinator of her congregation, who was deeply impressed by what she saw.

"Dorothy borrowed a Volkswagen to show me a bit of the town of Altamira," she wrote later. "After which I was taken to her 'home away from home,' a well-worn building with four walls and a roof. This little house was designed for the country people to use when they were in town for the night. The shower and latrine was out-of-doors in the enclosed yard—the term 'garden' would be a little ambitious to describe this bit of land. We left next morning at 6:45 after a piece of fresh bread and a cup of coffee. These bus rides are challenging experiences! About halfway to Nazaré the bus emptied so that it could be driven onto the ferry; on the other side we reentered the bus for the rest of the journey and arrived covered in dust. The area where Dot lives was cut out of the forest four years ago; it's hard to imagine its primitive nature. When we arrived, Sandra, one of the women who lives in the house, had made very fine white bread to welcome us, and what a treat it was. The community is made up of Dorothy and two young women, Isabel and Sandra, both supported by a California parish. The house is built of mud, and though it seems to me quite poor, Dot says you should have seen it before. She has succeeded in cultivating fruit and coffee trees and various bushes in the sand to beautify the land and provide some food as well. The chickens move freely in and out, and I had the dubious privilege of having one of the hens lay an egg under my hammock one morning.

"Dorothy battles her way through the bush, struggling to help the poor acquire a piece of land from which they can eke out a very modest living. The big landowners are enormously wealthy, and anyone who gets across them for any reason is under constant threat. It may look as though violence in Brazil is on the back burner, but the stark reality is quite otherwise: the victims of violence are the poor, the helpless, and those who try to help them. For twenty-seven years our sisters have aligned themselves with the peasants, whose only fault is to try to get enough land to feed their families, and sometimes when they return to their own countries for a well-earned rest we wonder why they have so changed. They cannot but be changed by the tragedies they see each day.

"Dorothy is well aware that she is on the list of troublemakers (read communists), but she is forced by poverty and injustice to risk her life in order to help the poor and landless. I was privileged to accompany her to a meeting of one of the base communities, and was deeply touched to have a family welcome us to supper before the meeting began. The main object of the meeting was to discover what they should charge for the use of their truck, and how they could pay back the money borrowed in even leaner times. The meeting was interrupted briefly when a very large tarantula crawled through an opening in the wall just behind my left shoulder. It was quickly disposed of and the meeting was resumed as though someone had spotted a harmless mosquito."

In March 1990 the mission office in Dayton received a disturbing letter from Sister Dorothy. For years she had been trying to get title to the plot of land where they had built the center at Nazaré. They had understood it to belong to the prelacy, but all of a sudden they had learned that the land commissioner had assigned the land to one of their neighbors. They were told that there was nothing to be done, and an offer by the neighbor to let them keep a small piece of land was withdrawn after he was told that the people in Nazaré were all communists. A surveyor had appeared while Dot was visiting one of the rural communities, and they were convinced that they would be evicted. Dot spent two weeks running around trying to find some solution to their problem, and it was at this point that a $900 check arrived from St. Raphael's in Ohio. Ecstatically, Dot wrote, "We want you to know that you are Divine Providence in action." They

planned to buy a piece of land about a mile away, dismantle the
two dorms, the church, and the sisters' house, and move to the
new property, but as things turned out they were able to prove
that the land did indeed belong to the prelacy of Xingu and had
been duly documented by the Land Agency.

Later that year there was a flutter of excitement as an agricultural technician named Gustavo came to visit from Austria,
at the invitation of Bishop Erwin. The Pioneer Association was
keen to hire a technician, and the community held its breath,
hoping they could persuade him to stay. Sadly for them, he decided to return to Austria, and the community suffered a double
loss sometime later when Sandra, one of the young women living with Dorothy, elected to follow him.

Nineteen ninety was another year of achievements. Padre Beto
came from Marabá to give a liturgy course and help the community think through ways of making their masses more alive and
relevant to the people's lives. Seminarian Paulo gave a drama
course. First communions were held in the rural communities.
Twenty-eight teachers completed their training, and the community threw a party to celebrate, transforming the men's dorm
into a party room. The bishop presided at mass, and Valdilene
cooked an armadillo for the occasion.

The year whirled past in a blur of meetings and visits, and
before Dot knew where she was, it was time to dispatch the first
batch of young people to the neighboring state of Macapá to
train as agricultural technicians, to celebrate the arrival of a new
VW Beetle, and then to head off to the States on a leave of absence. She took with her some videos of life in the communities,

and reported that she was getting pretty handy with the camcorder donated by a parish in Ohio. Her strategy was to allow the people to document their own stories, and film nights in the forest, powered by the car generator, were always great events, enthusiastically attended.

On May 22, 1991, Dorothy wrote to a family member in the United States, "Well, I'm celebrating my sixty years young and twenty-five of them in Brazil. Just want to shout to the world that they've been good and you've in some way helped to make them meaningful to me, as well as the great family I married into at age seventeen, Notre Dame. That I've been able to live, love, be loved, and work with the Brazilian people, help them find real confidence in themselves, to profoundly sense God's presence in their lives and then be a creative influence in society from which a more humane society can be born I thank you."

But life in the rain forest wasn't always a bed of roses. "I had the luck to be bitten by a mosquito that carries dengue," she added wryly. "I've had twelve malarias but one dengue won the prize."

Twenty-five years on the front line had taken its toll on her health, and the congregation was anxious for her to take time out to restore her energies and refresh her spirit. So in November 1991 she went back to the United States for a six-month sabbatical and gratefully accepted the offer to attend a course on creation spirituality. It was to be a revelation and a major turning point in her life.

ELEVEN

CREATION SPIRITUALITY

On previous trips to the States, Dot had conscientiously visited the mother house as well as her large extended family and friends, raised money for her work, and taken care of any health issues that might have arisen. But on this occasion the sisters and her family were concerned about her. They felt she deserved a break and the chance to get completely away from the strains and stresses of life in Brazil and ground herself once again. So they arranged for her to enroll for a semester's course on creation-centered spirituality at the University of the Most Holy Name in California.

It was a wonderful period for her, releasing her femininity and her artistic self and proving to be one of the pivotal events of her life. It was an opportunity to reevaluate the source of her strength, to lay aside, for the moment, the social activism that had consumed her, and to immerse herself in God's creation in all its abundance: people, plants, animals, water, air, and the good earth itself.

She had been raised in the old-style hierarchical church, where power was vested in the priests and absolute power was vested in the Pope, who was considered to be God's representative on earth and who spoke at times God's infallible truth. Nuns provided free labor for the church, and laypeople who obeyed the rules were assured of eternal salvation. All non-Catholics were effectively beyond the pale. As a sister of Notre Dame, Dorothy had submitted herself to the disciplines of chastity, poverty, and obedience, she had sublimated her womanhood by caring for the children of other women, and she had faced the twentieth century in the dress and customs of the eighteenth.

Despite the reforms of Vatican II, the church was still a hierarchical institution dominated by men. The ordination of women priests was resolutely opposed, and although nuns were given far greater autonomy than before, they continued to be subordinate to the priests. Among the laity, some women were beginning to occupy places as catechists and lay workers, but society told them from their earliest years that they were dependent on their men. Dot had looked at the peasant women and seen people who still possessed something of their ancestral wisdom, whose gifts were those of nurturing: children, families, and the earth. She saw people who had been dominated for centuries by their fathers, their husbands, their church, and their state, and she saw the potential waiting to be called forth. For twenty-five years, in the pursuit of social justice, she had worked with the landless to help them make a livelihood. And for twenty-five years the same pattern had been repeated: the forest had been felled, the earth had been degraded, and the families had been forced to sell up and move on. The old ways were not working, and a new way must be found.

In California she had the luxury of immersing herself in a whole new concept of spirituality, which had little to do with the tradition in which she had been raised. The image of God as the stern father of the Old Testament was transformed into the image of God as the Mother/Father of justice, compassion, and wisdom—Sophia. This new way of perceiving God was in direct contrast to the rigid teachings of the traditional Roman Catholic hierarchy, with its repression of the female. The male image of God as portrayed in the Bible, the emphasis on original sin, salvation through redemption, and the concept of redemptive violence were set against the female attributes of godhead: wisdom, justice, and compassion. Instead of seeking religion, God's people were to seek spirituality, echoing the words of Dietrich Bonhoeffer: "Jesus does not call us to a new religion but to life." God was in every part of this life, in every part of creation, and God's people were to live life abundantly, to fulfill their divine destiny as sons and daughters of God, and to work together to usher in the new reign of justice and compassion throughout the cosmos, bringing all things into harmony with the Creator.

This way of valuing the feminine brings Western thought in line with indigenous ways of valuing Mother Earth, revisiting biblical concepts of stewardship in terms of conservation rather than domination. Wise stewardship and conservation of our resources lead to righteousness, justice, and fair sharing, ensuring an abundant future for the planet and all its inhabitants for generations to come. This concept resonated strongly with Dot's most deeply held convictions, as she later confirmed in one of her letters: "Only a profound change in our way of living—our values and attitudes—can bring new life to our world."

Not that the concept of the feminine aspects of godhead was entirely new to the Western world. The Old Testament contains over four hundred references to the spirit of God in its female form, using the Hebrew word *ruach*. By the time the Scriptures were translated into Greek, the word used was *pneuma* (neuter), and in the Latin codices the word became male, *spiritus*. Yet we read in the New Testament that Jesus went out of his way to befriend women, who were considered inferior to men, that many of Jesus's followers were women, and that women helped to finance the early journeys of Jesus and his disciples. But as the hierarchy developed, early churchmen considered the very notion of associating spirituality with the female to be dangerously reminiscent of the ancient goddess religions and firmly repressed it. The Fall had come about through Eve; women were sinful and must live in subordination to men. Those who had the temerity to cling to old ways—for example, using their traditional knowledge of healing plants—were branded as witches and burned at the stake. Any form of dissent was rigidly punished by the Inquisition, and centuries later, in the 1980s and 1990s, the office of the Inquisition (renamed Congregation of the Doctrine of the Faith), in the person of Cardinal Ratzinger—now Pope Benedict XVI—continued to silence priests who espoused any form of theology that differed from the Vatican party line.

In the case of the Dominican brother Matthew Fox, who established the course that Dot attended, the cardinal's chief objection was that he was a feminist theologian who referred to God as Mother, who referred to original blessing instead of original sin, who associated too closely with Native American religions, who did not condemn homosexuality, and who had come up with a whole new concept of the spiritual journey. Traditionally the church had portrayed man's pilgrimage through the vale of tears to eternal life as requiring purgation from sin, illumination, and union with God. Matthew Fox and his fellow scholars turned that theology on its head. Instead of starting with the premise of original sin, they began with the doctrine of original blessing: God created the universe and saw that it was good. "Together we can make a difference," wrote Dot joyfully, "bringing peace, joy, caring, love to our world that is losing sight of our guiding star—the goodness of the real God."

Creation theology talks of four paths to perfection. The *via positiva* emphasizes wonder, awe, and rejoicing in all of God's creation. The *via negativa* is the shadow side, where we find darkness, silence, suffering, and letting go of self, all of which are equally real parts of our spiritual journey. Once we have experienced and embraced both light and darkness, we can set out along the *via creativa*, where we call forth the gifts inherent in God's creation and work to bring about the kingdom of God. And finally this leads to the *via transformativa*, where God's creation is restored through justice, compassion, harmony, and a new understanding of the interdependence of all life on the planet. And so the circle is completed.

Dot arrived in California shortly after Matthew Fox had

been expelled from the Dominican order, although he continued to teach. (His program was subsequently transferred to Wisdom University in Oakland.) Her work had been focused on activism; there had been little time for anything else. Yet she knew that what Fox taught was correct: that while spirituality without activism was arid intellectualism, activism without spirituality had effect but little depth. What is needed, he taught, is a radical fusion of spirituality and activism that enriches our spirit and transforms our activism. This can be achieved by a return to the ancient spiritual practices of mysticism, allied with wise use of modern science to bring about social and environmental welfare and revitalize Christianity. Creation spirituality is about the end of theism and the science of panentheism, which teaches that the image of God is immanent in all things but that God transcends the created order and permeates all things, and that Christ is God's liberating and reconciling energy which transforms individuals, institutions, and society. It's about trusting nature, including our own human nature, our dreams, our bodies, and our imaginations. It advocates that passion is a blessing rather than a curse; it emphasizes creativity over blind obedience, the aesthetic over the ascetic. It's about cosmology, placing the human agenda in touch with the cosmos.

It all begins with original blessing instead of original sin. God created the world and saw that it was good. Traditional teaching says that sin arises from disobedience to God's laws; creation theology says it comes from disconnectedness to God's creation. Instead of seven deadly sins—gluttony, sloth, lust, pride, envy, anger, and greed—it proposes seven principles of creation: cosmology, feminism, liberation, compassion, prophecy, creativity, and community. Instead of emphasizing redemption, creation theology stresses human connections to the cosmos. Instead of the historical Jesus, the cosmic Christ. Think positive: awe, wonder at the beauty of God's creation. Reconceive the universe as the mystical body of Christ. Reject patriarchal religion and reverence God as mother, Earth as mother, the universe as grandmother, drawing all religions together.

The basic tenets of this theology are these: Every human being is both mystic and prophet, and the universe is basically good. Yet all humans need to discover their true selves, and this journey consists of the fourfold way. As sons and daughters of God, we are all artists capable of creation; we are all part of the cosmos; we experience the divine as father as well as mother, child as well as parent. God is in all things, and all things are in God.

Dorothy was living an Old Testament life, where people tilled the soil, planted and harvested, looked after animals, and depended on one another for survival in a hostile environment. She was living among people who for the most part were intensely religious but at the same time had lost their primary bonds with the earth. They depended on it for their living, but they were a migrant race who regarded the forest as an enemy to be conquered, unlike the indigenous or traditional peoples, who had worked out ways of living with the forest and caring for it.

Dot had seen over and over how hopeful families cut and burned and planted and harvested and moved on because they didn't know how to care for the soils, which were quickly exhausted and could no longer sustain them. Instead of loving and reverencing the earth, they lived in fear. Fear of wild animals, snakes, poisonous spiders. Fear of the huge trees that towered overhead and kept out the sunlight. Fear of the indigenous people, who were strange and different. Fear of their fellow men, who coveted their lands and menaced them with guns. They needed to create a new relationship with the earth and with each other—a relationship in which men and women were prized and valued equally, children were welcomed and cherished, and that which was different could be seen and valued as part of the marvelous biodiversity of creation. "God's gift to us," she wrote, "is to live more fully as part of our cosmic creation."

She realized that the women and girls were especially needy—that they needed to be affirmed, allowed access to education and freedom, challenged to be everything that they could be. So she resolved to do everything in her power to help them feel at home in their wonderful forest, to care for it, understand it, and love it. To celebrate the gifts of life, the seedtime and harvest, the sunshine and rain, the light and darkness. To free themselves from dependence, to become strong and believe in themselves and their potential as daughters of God. To free not only themselves but also their men, who struggled under their own burdens.

Dot resolved that when she went back to Brazil, she would work with the women as well as the men to make their farms more productive, and she would do all she could to bring people to understand their part in creation—to show them that the better they cared for the land, the better it would care for them. "We must make great efforts to save our planet," she wrote. "Earth is not able to provide any more. Her water and air are poisoned and her soil is dying."

Dot had now spent eighteen years in Pará working with the settlers to secure their lands and livelihoods, and while there had been many successes, she had seen too many failures. It was becoming increasingly clear to her that the traditional practices of slash-and-burn agriculture were unsustainable and that a totally new way of working with the land was needed. She was determined to accept her shared responsibility to protect and restore the earth, and when she returned to Brazil in June 1992, her deepest convictions were strengthened when she attended the United Nations Conference on Environment and Development, also known as the Earth Summit. As she joined with half a million environmentalists from across the world who had come to Rio to debate better ways of caring for the planet, she could not have helped but resonate with the Earth Charter drawn up by the NGO conference participants. This is what it says:

> *We are Earth, the people, plants, and animals*
> *rains and oceans,*
> *breath of the forest and flow of the sea.*
> *We honor Earth as the home of all living things.*
> *We cherish Earth's beauty and diversity of life.*
> *We welcome Earth's ability to renew as being the basis of all*
>   *life.*
> *We recognize the special place of Earth's Indigenous Peoples,*
> *Their territories, their customs,*
> *And their unique relationship to Earth.*
> *We are appalled at the human suffering, poverty, and*
> *damage to Earth*
> *caused by inequality of power.*
> *We accept a shared responsibility to protect and*
> *restore Earth*

And to allow wise and equitable use of resources
So as to achieve an ecological balance
And new social, economic and spiritual values.
In all our diversity we are one.
Our common home is increasingly threatened.

TWELVE

PUTTING CREATION SPIRITUALITY TO WORK

After the Earth Summit, Dot returned to Nazaré with her head brimming with ideas. Her team had now expanded: postulants Isabel, Sandra, and Rita had been joined by Maria dos Santos and Waldiria. "We covered all the country roads," says Maria dos Santos. "We'd be out for three or four days at a time, and we'd cut across through the forest between one road and the next so that we didn't have to go all the way back to the highway." In an explosion of energy, the communities organized a women's group, made and sold clothes to raise money, established cooperatives for hulling rice and grinding corn, and started discussing plans to build a fruit processing factory powered by electricity generated by a small dam. Inspired by her grounding in creation spirituality, Dot painted T-shirts with ecological slogans—*The Death of the Forest Is the Death of Us All*—and a picture of the forest alive with divine beings. "She truly believed that God was in all things," said one of the sisters later. "And she felt enormous pain when she'd see a mahogany tree burned to the ground."

By November 1992 there was no sign of rain, the heat was terrific, and there were fires on all sides. But people were beginning to think in a new way and were talking about planting trees instead of cutting them. They also decided that one of their most urgent needs was some reliable form of transport to carry their produce to the highway, and they were overjoyed to learn that the parish of St. Raphael's would fund the purchase of a 50-horsepower tractor and trailer. The equipment would take several months to reach them but was to be in service by the middle of 1993.

But things did not work out as projected, because of three factors: economic instability, lack of financial planning, and miscommunication. Against a background of high inflation and increasing difficulty in figuring out their costs, the community at Nazaré decided to reassign funds without first consulting the parish in Ohio. The tractor arrived in Altamira, but the state of the road meant that it could not reach Nazaré until after the rains in June. And in the meantime the community decided to trade it for a truck, on the grounds that a truck would have greater carrying capacity, be better equipped to take the steep hills, and be more economical to run. They located a suitable vehicle with 50,000 miles on the clock, which they could trade for the unused tractor, and they were happy to report that the deal included a rice hulling machine, which would enable them

not only to get a better price for threshed rice but also to generate a supply of rice husks for animal feed.

Yet what seemed perfectly logical on the ground looked different from the parish office in Ohio. St. Raphael's had given
money for a tractor, and they wanted to know why they hadn't
got a tractor. Dorothy, who seldom used a typewriter, much less
a computer, was obliged to enter upon a long and occasionally
testy handwritten correspondence over the course of many
months. She explained that Brazil was in a period of high inflation and that the cost of freight would no longer cover running
expenses, which was why the community had decided on a
truck.

The parish office pointed out that a truck had more moving
parts than a tractor and would break down more often. If the
people in Ohio had had any idea of what 50,000 miles on those
roads would do to a truck, they might well have been even more
irritable. They wanted to know whether a truck would give better mileage than a tractor and whether the community would be
able to use it more profitably.

Dorothy sat down and wrote them a long letter, explaining
that the problem had been a lack of adequate planning but that
the economic situation had taken everyone by surprise. "Why
didn't we calculate all this before?" she wrote. "Good question.
We are working with the poorest of the poor, who have never
administered anything. One has one idea, another has another,
and we are many. We try to listen to each one and act on the
knowledge that we have."

The parish officials told her that they didn't like the idea of
changing the tractor for a truck. A tractor would operate more
efficiently and reliably over difficult roads. But, they concluded,

it was important for them to trust her and grant her the right to be wrong.

And there, no doubt to their mutual relief, the correspondence ended.

In the sultry, sweaty months of October and November 1994, Dot sent a letter to her family that hinted at the frustration and exhaustion she was beginning to feel as the years rolled by. "It is so hot here that I'd love to be a fish in cool water instead of my sweat," she wrote, and then, in an uncharacteristic mood of depression, "We're getting older and I get tired of fighting for better times. If they come, they come." But she rallied quickly, reminding herself and her friends that "our Church will rumble along but God in all Her goodness is Eternal! I realize that all of you also live in a world full of contradictions and try to bring your contributions so that new life is constantly being born. If I've helped, thank God; if at times I've been a stone in your shoe, forgive me. Just want to say that life doesn't stop at sixty and I still need your friendship to give me energy as at times I feel that the ole gray mare she ain't what she used to be and I do so still want to be a part of it all."

Around this time Dot was becoming increasingly involved in local politics, and community efforts were rewarded in 1995 when the state government acceded to their request to create a new county based in the town of Anapu, some twenty miles from Nazaré. In Brazil, political power is traditionally held in the cities and the rural areas are left to their own devices, so the prospect of becoming a new county was very enticing, provided that the people could elect a hardworking and honest mayor

and council. The new county would also be eligible for federal start-up funds to improve roads, schools, and health care. It would be large. "We are 100 km [60 miles] in extension and an average of 70 km [44 miles] in width," Dot wrote. "The area has been abandoned by our two former county seats. What political wrangling to break loose! We've been at it since 1988—it's a long hard slog."

The creation of a new county, which went into effect in 1996, acted as an incentive to new migrants, and Dot found herself increasingly concerned about the families that arrived week after week. Her main focus was on helping them find land and new ways of living sustainably, and it seemed logical for her team to move from the tiny settlement of Nazaré to the more central location of Anapu, first port of call for many of the arriving families.

The following year the primitive parish house in Anapu was knocked down and replaced with a beautiful new wooden house with cement floors and running water. By comparison with the house in Nazaré, it was positively luxurious, and Dot reveled in the novelty of running water and a telephone. On September 28, 1997, a mass was held to consecrate the foundation stone for the new church, and amid rising excitement the building materials were assembled. In December the old wooden church was demolished and the space cleared for the most important event of the decade, the ordination of three young *padres*, one of whom, Padre Amaro, would stay and work in the parish.

It was a huge celebration. They were expecting hundreds of people, and the preparations took many weeks. People came from far and wide to help out. One of the loggers lent his truck to help clean up after the church was demolished, and the helpers were rewarded with popcorn. Benches were constructed out of tree stumps supplied by the mayor and planks on loan from the sawmill, a shelter was erected over the cooking area to keep the cooks dry, and somebody had the forethought to install a privy.

"We had about 1,500 people from some 50 small communities," wrote Dot, "and some 500 from other areas of the prelacy—priests, seminarians, and friends from around the state. In order to feed them all we asked the communities to send us rice, beans, cornmeal, manioc, coffee, chickens, and pig meat. Somebody even sent us a cow!

"We are united with four other faith traditions," she continued, "Baptist, Assembly of God, Adventists, and *macumba*, all coming together as a great witness to our unity and strength." On January 31, 1998, the square was packed in honor of the ordination. A dance offering celebrated the fruits of the earth—cornmeal cakes, blocks of raw brown sugar, delicious crumbly manioc cookies—and in the Afro-Brazilian mass, Amaro's parents ritually presented their son to the bishop. It was wonderful to see everyone celebrating together and bringing their gifts to the altar. "But the greatest gift of all," Dot pointed out, "is the gift of our lives."

As they cleared away after the festivities, they little guessed that their next undertaking was to demand every ounce of energy and determination, strain their resources to the utmost, and bring them in turn to the mountaintop and to the valley of the shadow of death. But all that lay ahead.

Anapu was a run-down little settlement when Dot first arrived, and although its population has expanded explosively, it still isn't much of a place. A straggling township of wooden buildings, it crouches on the edge of the Transamazon Highway, waiting for better times. It's a gritty Amazon town with shabby trading posts selling secondhand clothing, hammocks, and bottles of liquor, with music pounding out from every corner, motorbikes roaring along the dusty streets, blowing litter, open drains, whirling dust, huge logging trucks, beat-up VW buses piled with boxes and bundles, and people always on the move to the next town, to the rutted roads of the interior. The town sprawls in a disorderly fashion up the hill to the warehouse where the mayor keeps the road machines and members of the city council sit on uncomfortable chairs in their air-conditioned meeting room, past the brand-new Farm Workers' Union with the armed guard seated outside, to the empty building that housed the community radio until the mayor closed it down. An ugly concrete park sits on an island in the middle of the highway, but nobody stops to rest on its broken benches and no children play on the rusty swings in the playground. Below the highway, the smart new church stands next to the simple wooden buildings that house the parish hall and the *padre*'s house.

Over the thirty years of the town's existence, the original mud houses with earth floors have been replaced by wooden houses with cement floors, wood shingles have been replaced by tiles, and a telephone tower has come to dominate the skyline. The mayor has built schools, a small hospital, and a police station, and a miscellaneous assortment of trading houses, sawmills, mechanics' shops, gas stations, bars, lodging houses, and brothels has crept in both directions along the corrugated highway that leads to the distant cities of Altamira to the west and Pacajá to the east.

Behind the church a small path leads to the banks of the Anapu River. Women crouch on the rocks, rhythmically slapping their clothes in the water, and children swim in the pools, oblivious of the sewage that flows directly into the river. A swaying wooden bridge leads to the opposite bank, where one of the more ambitious settlers is building a nightclub and a swimming pool. A narrow path winds through a patch of high forest to a clearing where the parish has constructed the São Rafael Training Center: simple wooden dormitories, a circular meeting house, and a roofed classroom.

The training center has been years in the making. The area was first cleared in 1991 by a youth group from kilometer 120. In the early days there was no bridge, and all the building supplies came in by canoe. A few weeks later wooden roofing shingles were cut for the first house. The building progressed slowly, depending on the availability of manpower and money. In 1993 the community built the kitchen and the circular meeting place, and in the following year the men's dormitory, with room for fifty hammocks. In 1995 the kitchen got a tiled roof, the circular building got a cement floor, and stone arrived for a new women's dormitory, which was completed in January 1996. São Rafa, as it was christened, became the site of constant activity, with regular meetings of the Pioneer Association, women, youth, farmers, the planning committee, and Bible students.

But despite all the progress, violence was never far from the surface, and in a letter to the mission office dated November 1995, Dot described it as "never diminishing, it's intensifying, just changing methods. Drugs are a constant problem, public forest land is being pillaged for hardwoods, and ranchers are cutting and burning as fast as they can." She describes an area of forest that had been recently cleared: "1,000 hectares [2,500 acres] at one burning. Smoke hung in the air for days.

"Umberto is one of the Precious Blood brothers who came to the small town of Altamira in 1956 when it was surrounded by Indian reservations," she continues. "He set up a small printing press, and used his mechanical skills for working on motors for boats, cars, trucks, and lumber mills. He was a very simple man and quiet. On 10th October he answered the doorbell at our diocesan center in Altamira and two men entered and shot him dead. We later heard they were looking for Father Frederic Scheel."

Once the new county of Anapu was safely launched and the new church buildings were planned, Dot's irrepressible energies were directed once more to the question of the fruit processing factory. Her letters describe how the community was looking for government support to build a small, 95-kilowatt dam during the dry season to provide power not only for processing fruit but also for a woodworking shop and a cheese factory. In the meantime the women were working with medicinal plants, the men were starting to plow with oxen, and they were planting mahogany and cedar trees. "Working with forest land is very delicate," she says. "How are we to help the people recapture a relationship with Mother Earth that is tender and kind?"

As the months passed, the five-year-old dream of the fruit factory moved with excruciating slowness. Machinery was donated by a foundation in Luxembourg, but no progress was made on the dam, and it was rapidly becoming a standing joke—rather, as Dot wrote, like Noah building the ark before the flood.

But, she continued indomitably, the factory would "revolution-ize our whole financial structure. The people will have a place to sell what they produce and hopefully this fruit can be processed and exported."

In February 1997 the new two-room school was completed at Nazaré, and work on building the fruit factory finally started. The community turned out to collect stones for the foundation, Father Frederic sent them 8,000 bricks, a well was financed by a small nonprofit based in Belém, and machinery was installed. The machines would process fruits grown by the settlers, and the pulp would be frozen and sold for juice.

In July three young men graduated as agricultural techni-cians and started to share their newly acquired skills with the communities. "They are bringing us more creative farming in keeping with our Amazon environment, together with organiza-tional skill," Dot wrote. "What a feeling of achieving! I feel I can sit back a bit now and enjoy the enthusiasm they bring."

In 1998 work on the long-awaited dam finally began, despite threats from a neighboring farmer, Antonio Vicente, that he would blow it up. But the construction proceeded slowly, and before the workers could complete the dam, they had to build a bridge to transport the building materials. After the bridge was finally built, it was swept away in a flood. The community re-built it, but Vicente kept his word and burned it down.

Faced with a serious shortfall of funding to complete the fruit factory, Dot prepared a handwritten proposal asking for $30,000 and submitted it to the parish office in Dayton, explain-ing that the project had the potential to transform the area. "We're becoming aware of our tremendously environmentally rich forest with all its biodiversity," she added. "Instead of relying on slash and burn to produce rice and beans, exhausting soil fertility and totally destroying the biodiversity, we can produce tropical fruits."

Dot ended with a retrospective of what had been achieved to date. "Beginning in '83 we started to organize small one-room schools and bring teachers from Belém to train our women as teachers. We now have fifty-six schools going to the fourth grade and six going to eighth grade. For fifteen years we have been working with local plants and now have some twenty women involved in using natural methods to cure our ills. We're also involved in community projects, planting coffee, cocoa, pepper, and hardwoods. We ask your help so that we can complete the construction and be able to start processing the fruits: indigenous fruits to start with—*açai, bacaba, cupuaçu, graviola*—these have immediate marketing potential. We are full of life and hope in our desire to bring a better standard of living to our struggling families, to ensure a better future in the third millennium."

But larger forces were at work, and while Dorothy and her people dreamed of creating a successful model of family agriculture, planners in government offices in Brasília were reviving an old dream of Amazon development. This dream relied not so much on the huge expanses of land as on the rivers, with their potential to generate immense amounts of electricity to power heavy industry to exploit the vast mineral resources that lay beneath the forest floor.

The first sign of this was the announcement by the federal government of the construction of a gigantic dam on the River Xingu, projected to generate 11,000 megawatts of electricity.

This project had been in the works since 1975, when the state electricity company, Eletronorte, had hired a team of consultants to examine the feasibility of constructing a series of dams on the Xingu. Four years later they had come up with a study projecting five possible dam sites on the Xingu and the Iriri, to be named after the indigenous groups in whose traditional lands they were to be built: Kararao, Babaquara, Ipixuna, Kokraimoro, and Jarina. Initial resistance to the project came to a head during the First Meeting of the Indigenous Nations of the Xingu, held in Altamira in 1989, when, amid vociferous protests, one of the indigenous women, Tu Ira, waved a machete in the face of the chief engineer, José Antonio Muniz Lopes. The project was temporarily shelved.

But if the battle was won, the war was far from over. Ten years later the project surfaced again, in a different form. Eletronorte's new publicity campaign was aimed at winning hearts and minds. The location of the dam was moved to avoid direct confrontation with the small indigenous population. The project was renamed Belo Monte, local schoolchildren and leaders were wooed with excursions to visit the existing dam at Tucurui, and a smart new cultural center was built on the waterfront in Altamira, providing computer access and an architectural model of the dam.

Huge construction projects like Belo Monte require an enormous workforce, and the immediate consequences of resurrecting the project were both predictable and disastrous. The smallest suggestion of large numbers of jobs was enough to attract hordes of migrants from the northeast, who came swarming along the Transamazônica into the existing settlements in search of the jobs that had not yet materialized. With no prospect of employment, they had little alternative but to search for a piece of land so they could feed their families.

It was at exactly this moment that the Amazon Development Agency, SUDAM, which had been inactive for several years, chose to revive its program of financing large-scale projects, with the result that businessmen, loggers, and land speculators came tumbling in from all sides. Competition for the land suddenly became intense, and the stage was set for land conflicts of a violence and intensity that had never been seen in the region.

THIRTEEN

THE LAND WARS

As the land conflicts escalated, they spawned a whole new cast of characters. First came the large landowners: businessmen, loggers, ranchers, dealers in agricultural products, and politicians either from the region or from farther afield. They were (and are) supported by their private cohorts of thugs and gunmen, members of the military police or security firms who manned the guard-posts and patrolled the boundaries, and reinforced by those who dealt in land documentation: notaries public, real estate agents, lawyers, topographers, and fraudsters offering land for sale on the Internet. It's a long-established industry, an open secret that few people dare to confront. A widely circulated but unsigned list of known land grabbers in the Anapu region in 1998 gives names, areas of activity, and estimated category of dangerousness:

Avelino Dedeia *Residence: Anapu. Active in: Esperança Project. Involved in: pistolagem (use of gunmen). Extremely dangerous.*

JK *Residence: Anapu. Involved in: pistolagem, land grabbing. Extremely dangerous.*

Reinaldo Zucatelli *Residence: Marabá. Active in: Belo Monte. Involved in: pistolagem. Highly dangerous.*

Peixoto *Residence: Anapu, Altamira. Active in: Bacajá. Highly dangerous.*

Efraim *Residence: Anapu. Active in: Manduacari. Involved in: pistolagem. Highly dangerous.*

Franklin Penteado *Residence: Anapu. Active in: Belo Monte, Bacajá. Highly dangerous.*

Délio Fernandes *Residence: Anapu. Involved in: sale of public lands, deforestation, and financial fraud. Highly dangerous.*

Davi Resende *Residence: Altamira. Active in: Manduacari. Involved in: pistolagem, drug trafficking. Dangerous.*

Luis Ungaratti *Active in: Bacajá. Involved in: stealing timber. Dangerous.*

Regivaldo (aka Taradão) *Residence: Altamira. Involved in: money-lending, money laundering, financing political campaigns. Dangerous.*

Regivaldo was a prominent businessman living in Altamira. Although he dabbled in land speculation and was convicted and fined heavily for maintaining slave laborers on a farm in the

Anapu region, his main business was lending money to land-owners who had incurred debts in dealing with SUDAM, and he was well known for charging exorbitant interest—up to 30 percent. Although neither he nor Dorothy knew it, their fates were to be closely linked as Dot began to acquire a reputation as a defender of the settlers and later when she was accused of supplying them with arms and inciting violence. It all started with the case of the Manduacari ranch, or *fazenda*.

The first land concessions on Fazenda Manduacari had been taken up as long before as 1974. In those days it was a condition of the concessions that if the land wasn't developed within five years, it would return to the federal government, and since this area had never been put under production, the concessions had been canceled—in theory. In practice the government usually neglected to take any steps, with the result that in many cases concessions were sold on to other landowners, sometimes in good faith and sometimes in the hope that nobody would notice. By 1999 none of the original claimants to the land was still in residence.

On December 12, 2002, three hundred families moved into the area and started to clear land for their lots, on the understanding that the land had now reverted to the government. No sooner had they begun to clear the land and build their houses than they heard that a man named Yoaquim Petrola de Melo was claiming 37,500 acres known as Fazenda Cospel, which included the land on which they had settled. They had hardly digested this unwelcome information when Yoaquim himself arrived to evict them, escorted by a heavily armed force of military police and gunmen. The eviction was as violent as it was unexpected: men were beaten, houses were burned with all their contents, and everyone was loaded onto a cattle truck to be sent to Anapu. Six of the settlers were arrested, jailed on trumped-up charges, and held for four months without trial. The word on the street was that Yoaquim had hired a couple of known gunmen (including JK, who was listed as "extremely dangerous") and had paid 80,000 reais (around US$22,000 at that time) to the police in order to get the job done.

For nine months the families stayed off the land, missing the planting season and making a living as best they could. Meanwhile the Farm Workers' Union, the Pastoral Lands Commission, the *padres*, and the sisters mounted a campaign to publicize the situation, and in September 2003 their efforts were rewarded by the arrival in Anapu of the national ombudsman for agricultural affairs, who reviewed the settlers' case and recommended resettlement. On the strength of this, and anxious to prepare the ground for the next planting season, 153 families moved back onto the land, after informing INCRA of their decision.

Four days later the battle began. Benedito, the farm manager on Fazenda Cospel, appeared, accompanied by a driver and a policeman, and started to threaten the settlers. This time they were better prepared, and Benedito was outnumbered, overpowered, and disarmed. The settlers delivered his weapons to the police station in Anapu, where Benedito registered a complaint that he had been robbed of 2,000 reais. The following day the local bureau chief of INCRA visited the area, declared that the land was not under production, and authorized the families to start planting. Over the course of the next year their lands were officially registered and they were informed that they qualified for food rations from the government. They first had to send a delegation to Anapu with the list of names, and then their troubles would be over.

When the settlers returned, they were surprised and alarmed to find that a chain had been put across the road and a guardpost erected, manned by sixteen highly armed guards. They were brusquely informed that they would have to leave the land as soon as possible. Deeply concerned, they hurried back to Anapu to inform the police, who promptly arrested two of their party. Disturbing rumors began to circulate: Benedito was promising to kill the ringleaders, the guards were armed with machine guns . . .

After a court hearing several months later, the settlers learned that Yoaquim's concessions were to be canceled and that he had been ordered to remove the guardpost and allow them free access. The courts could say what they wished, but in these lawless lands their word counted for little, and shortly afterward the settlers' houses were invaded once again and their possessions destroyed. But this time when the gunmen returned to complete the job, the settlers were prepared. Amid renewed invasions and burnings, there was a fierce shootout, during which both sides sustained injuries. The sides were drawn up and war was declared.

For a few days matters settled into an uneasy truce, but the situation was highly explosive, and it was only a matter of time before violence broke out once more. Yoaquim reinforced his guards, announcing that no one would be permitted to pass through his land, and his guards opened fire on a Volkswagen bus as it drove down the road. Shortly afterward several of the settlers contracted malaria, and when they attempted to get into town to buy medicine, they were repeatedly shot at and prevented from passing. A few days later they returned in force, and in the ensuing skirmish injuries were sustained on both sides and one of the guards was killed.

It was just the excuse the police needed to initiate a reign of terror in Anapu. Houses were invaded, doors broken down, documents confiscated, guns brandished. Arrests were made and people were severely beaten. The regional police chief announced that Dorothy's "guerrillas" had ambushed and killed one of Yoaquim's workers, and she was charged with inciting violence. "I've taken more of a front run on this," she wrote later, "because it is less likely that I will be harmed. I can be the voice for the people who would risk jail or worse. I can speak out."

The town continued to suffer under a spate of police savagery. The police picked up an old man on his way home from work, handcuffed him, and drove him to Manduacari, where they burned down his house along with several others and all their contents. Fifty-five women marched to the police station

to hold a candlelit vigil, but they were repulsed by twenty heavily armed policemen.

A lawyer arrived in town and accompanied Padre Amaro to the police station to inquire as to whether the police had search and arrest warrants. When he asked for copies of police documents, he was told that no copier was available. The police station emptied out, and an uneasy calm settled on the town. Everyone, both in Anapu and on Manduacari, was keeping a low profile.

A hearing was held in the town hall, where Gabriel from the Farm Workers' Union testified that the settlers had authorization from INCRA to remain on the land. A few days later the police invaded the area once again and burned down the houses. In the dark of night, Yoaquim's guardpost and some of his farm buildings were mysteriously burned to the ground. Nobody saw anything.

A second hearing was held, this time in the agricultural tribunal at Marabá, and Dot was summoned to respond to the allegation that she was providing food and arms to the families on Manduacari. She replied that she had indeed delivered government food rations to the settlers, but denied that she had ever encouraged them to use arms. But she did state that she didn't feel confident in asking for police help because she considered that the police were on the side of Yoaquim. It was an accusation that the local police chief would not forget.

From this period on, the focus of the settler communities shifted from schools and health, improved roads and transport, to the question of land—how to get it and how to keep it. The subject of land reform had been raised in 1994, before Anapu had become a county, but INCRA was underresourced and fundamentally unwilling to tackle what was politically a very hot potato. INCRA staff took refuge in vague promises that amounted to nothing, and in the meantime a steady trickle of families moved onto the backlands, where they were neither challenged nor affirmed.

In 1997 the Farm Workers' Union and the Pastoral Lands Commission, headed by Dorothy, registered a request with INCRA to set aside two areas for land reform—178,000 of the 1.25 million acres on the area known as Gleba Belo Monte for the Esperança Project, and 155,000 of the 520,000 acres on Gleba Bacajá for the project to be called Virola Jatobá. (Large areas of land in the Amazon are known as *glebas*.) Instead of the traditional model of land reform, these were to be projects of sustainable development (PDS in Portuguese), combining sustainable agriculture with conservation of the forest and a form of communal ownership of the land. INCRA agreed to their request, and Dorothy offered to do what she could to help by registering the names of potential settlers.

The difficulties were immense. There was a complex tapestry of land claims, many of which had been sold on. Titles had been transferred in the office of the notary public in Altamira, who was widely suspected of being dishonest and was later put out of business. The land was difficult to get to and hadn't been properly surveyed. It also contained some fine stands of mahogany, which was worth a lot of money to someone. The combination of powerful business interests, land-hungry peasants, and inept government oversight was a recipe for confusion, corruption, and conflict.

But the idea of sustainable development was a completely new approach to land reform, and one that aroused considerable interest among some Amazon observers, such as Carlos Mendes. As a journalist for newspapers in São Paulo and Belém, Mendes had been covering the land situation and specifically the land conflicts for over thirty years. "I'm an investigative journalist," he says, "the toughest branch of journalism. You have to look into things and you come up against the big economic interests—loggers, large landowners, and big corporations. It's a dangerous business here in Amazônia—I always say the paper ought to give us life insurance! I cover land conflicts, slave labor, illegal logging, invading indigenous areas, and stealing minerals and timber. The five mortal sins of Amazônia. Part of the fabric of Dorothy's life.

"She was organizing the settlers to get land—land reform. In the rest of the world nobody talks about land reform—it already happened long ago. But here in Brazil it's still a hot topic. And Sister Dorothy, at the age of seventy-three, was in it up to her neck.

"I first came across Dorothy when she was working in Jacundá back in the eighties, but I didn't really start to take an interest in her work until around 2002. It was one of the most intense periods of my life, because in Dorothy I found myself face-to-face with an energy, an interior strength, and an idealism that were absolutely captivating.

"She was a very special person, because her idea of land reform was very different from that of the experts. She wanted something quite different. Not just the classic land reform, transferring land title and abandoning the settlers. I always say that land reform the way it's done in Brazil is like making bean soup just using beans. If you want to make the soup taste good, you have to put in lots of other ingredients. The way the government does it, they dole out land titles and that's it. They don't give the settlers credit or roads or schools or health posts—they don't give them a life of dignity.

"And of course Dorothy came up against the powerful landowners, a race of people at once greedy, perverse, and backward. The only reason they want the land is so that they can knock down the forest. They don't even understand the principles of economics. They'd make far more money if the forest was still standing—selling carbon credits and using the forest's natural resources. But all they want to do is cut the trees, plant pasture, and raise cattle for export. There's no fair distribution of wealth. In fact, it's worse than that, because they still have slave labor on the cattle ranches. A peon can work all his life to make money for his boss, and when he's seventy years old he won't even have the right to a retirement pension.

"Dorothy never tired of talking about those projects of hers. She always traveled with a pile of documents, dog-eared, stained, beaten-up old papers that had been in and out of dozens of government offices. Where she always got the same response: 'Come back tomorrow, Sister Dorothy. Come back next week.'

"That's how they treated her—as if she was nobody. 'Wait outside,' they'd say—three hours, four hours, six hours sometimes. She used to look me up when she came to Belém and tell me what was going on in Anapu. 'Carlos,' she'd say, 'take a look at this.' And there's me, a journalist, fed up with seeing so many projects, and I'm thinking to myself, What kind of project can a seventy-year-old woman have come up with, for heaven's sake?

Because in this country, as you know, there's a tendency not to value older people. To put them on the shelf. But Sister Dorothy, with all her vitality—when she said she had a project, I said, 'Well now, what project is that?'

"Her project was the real thing. A genuine land reform. Way outside the league of the government authorities. The idea was to make the project sustainable. Not to cut everything that grew and plant grass everywhere, like they did in the south of Pará, where you can drive for miles and never see a single tree standing. The idea was that the settlers would use twenty percent of their land and keep the rest in forest reserve. They'd own the land, but if they wanted to leave they'd have to sell it to the association. That way the land would stay with smallholders and not get swallowed up by the big ranches, as happened in so many other places.

"And it was starting to work. No thanks to INCRA—it was Dorothy and her people who were getting the project off the ground. Real sustainable development. Good for the people, and good for the forest. Making sure that the land was productive. It has to be the way forward. It's a model that could be exported across the world, wherever there's standing forest.

"She was a visionary, you know. She was trying to prepare the people for what was going to happen in the future. Because it's going to be hard, and she could see that. It's not that she was a seer, but she was intuitive. And energy? I used to ask where she got her strength from. And she'd always smile and say, 'Well, Carlos, first from God and then from the people. From our people.' She always called them that. Not that they were her people, but that she was a part of them. And now I can see that she had her priorities absolutely right. I think that in twenty years' time she'll be remembered for her vision. In twenty years' time, when Amazônia has been destroyed even more, when the land wars are even more violent than they are now, people will remember her and say, 'Sister Dorothy was absolutely right.' "

FOURTEEN

SUSTAINABILITY: THE IMPOSSIBLE DREAM?

Felício, the federal prosecutor, takes up the story. "The idea in itself was a good one," he says. "And to start with, it looked like it might work out. But then, around 1999 or 2000, the question of the Belo Monte dam came up again. It was to be third largest in the world. The government only had to announce it and people came swarming into the area, mostly from the south of Pará and Maranhão. First the settlers and then right behind them the land grabbers, buying up land titles right, left, and center. It wasn't as if the dam was a reality—just an idea, and a crazy one at that. The whole project was full of mistakes. It wouldn't have generated even ten percent of what had been projected.

"But as it was, hordes of starving people from the northeast came streaming along the road, and most of them ended up in Anapu. And they'd go straight to the little green house next to the church, because they'd heard it was Dorothy's house. First off she'd find them some food, because they'd been traveling for days and they were famished. Then she'd fix them up with a place to sleep—that little hut in the yard, or else the parish hall. There were families living there for weeks on end.

"She knew there was public land available just thirty miles off the highway, and that's where she'd send the people. In other parts of Brazil you get the landless invading farmlands, but here it was the other way around—the small guys got here first. And Dorothy never sent anyone onto land that belonged to someone else. Only onto public land, land that had reverted to the government when the concessions had lapsed. Once they were settled, along would come the land grabber with a document in his hand saying that the land belonged to him. There was nothing on it—no farm buildings, no houses, no fencing, nothing. Just virgin forest."

"It was an impossible situation," adds Felício's colleague Ubiratan Cazetta. "On the one hand INCRA was encouraging smallholder settlement, and on the other SUDAM was financing large projects. Some of the settlers had been there for years, and all of a sudden they were getting expelled by those guys who claimed to hold concessions dating back to the seventies. What was worse was that INCRA upheld their claims, even though today most of them are the subject of court cases for fraud.

"And in this context you'll get some names coming up over and over again. Among them Regivaldo, known as Taradão. He's always associated with money-lending, although I don't think he personally had any financing from SUDAM. But he was hand in glove with plenty who did, including a bunch of politicians. Délio Fernandes, for example. [Fernandes was denounced for land grabbing on lots 56, 58, 60, 61, and 62 on Bacajá, but a local judge upheld his claim to the land. He was also alleged to have swindled SUDAM out of 5 million reais for a fictitious cocoa/cattle project.] In fact, even in those days, around 2000, that group was giving us cause for anxiety. My colleague Felício and I did our best to get INCRA to move ahead with the sustainable development projects, because something needed to be done urgently for the people who lived over there. It was the very worst stretch of the entire Transamazônica. And there was Dorothy, battling away to get a better life for the people. To avoid the mistakes that had been made in the south of Pará. To make sure that development went together with environmental protection. Because it was perfectly possible. She saw that clearly. And the amazing thing was that she was making it happen. As a model of land reform, it was both completely legal and totally sustainable.

"It always surprised me how she had the guts to live in such a difficult region. It's really terrible. When it rains there's mud everywhere, and when it's dry it's nothing but dust. How could she live there so long and actually seem to enjoy it? And she never stayed still. One minute she'd be in Belém, then she'd hop on the bus home with no idea of how long it would take, and then the very next week she'd be back here. The energy of the woman used to drive me wild! I just couldn't understand it, until one day I went to Anapu and I understood. She was completely fulfilled and happy there. She had found her mission.

"It was all public land. Yes, there had been concessions, but that was thirty years ago, and the land had reverted to the state. Some of those former owners had registered land titles, and some had sold their lots, but that was completely illegal. There was no one living there. So INCRA decided to set up this sustainable project—PDS, they called it—on exactly that land, and they said that any previous titles were worthless. But as people started coming into the area, the land values began to increase, and this guy Taradão managed to get title to some of the land. False, of course. Sold it to a fellow from Espírito Santo by the name of Bida, and he moved in and started clearing the land, right in the middle of the Esperança PDS. Sent his henchman Tato to threaten the settlers. INCRA took him to court, and the judge said he'd have to get off the land while the case was being decided, and the settlers could stay where they were. But of course he refused to budge, and INCRA couldn't make him. So the situation became very explosive."

While Carlos, Ubiratan, and Felício were unconditional fans of Dorothy's, they had known her for only a comparatively short time, while she was in the eye of the storm. Padre Nello, the rubicund Italian who works with the Indigenous Missionary Council, goes much farther back and has a somewhat different perspective.

"I first met Dorothy in 1968 in Coroatá," he says, "and I knew her when she worked in the prelacy of Marabá, but it wasn't until she moved onto the Transamazônica that she gave herself body and soul to the cause of the landless. It was a total dedication. But of course she could be very trying. As far as Dorothy was concerned, the sun rose and set around her people.

Anyone who came anywhere near got roped in to help. It was all Dorothy's people, Dorothy's people. You'd think that nobody else counted.

"I don't know where she got this passion for conservation. All those settlers on the PA 150, every last one from Maranhão, they thought of nothing but cutting the forest. They'd never dream of planting a tree! And this sustainable development project had been dreamed up by INCRA, but they'd never got it to work. It was Dorothy who really pushed for it. She truly thought it could be done. Nature became her gospel, you might say. Loving nature, preserving nature, because nature is life.

"And she sold the idea to the settlers, she really did. When you go onto the project and you talk about Dorothy, they'll show you a seedling and they'll say, 'Look, I planted this tree.' They're putting her gospel into practice. It was that obstinacy of hers, believing when everyone else was convinced it would fail. And at the end of the day she's achieving in death what she never would have achieved in life.

"She was working with people who had a completely different mentality. And she never rejected anyone, because she always said there was room for everyone, no matter who they were. Even though some of them caused her trouble. But she always maintained that they should have a chance, and she never distinguished between them. That was her downfall. She should have been more careful.

"The people went along with the whole idea, but she was the one who got things moving. She went around from pillar to post asking for money, getting hold of technicians to help out. And the most important thing is that she managed to convince the people, and the government, that there were better ways of using the land. And that's where the men who killed her lost out. Sometimes a project doesn't work from the point of view of making money, but it changes people's attitudes. If it serves to pull people together and get them thinking, then it's worth the effort.

"They needn't have killed her, you know. If things had kept on the way they were going, I doubt if the project would have worked out. If they'd been a bit more patient, she'd have been finished. She used to say, 'We're losing.' Not that she was disheartened, but she couldn't see the way forward. She had tried everything, and the settlers were giving up. Just a bit longer, and Tato would have won.

"But instead it was Dorothy who won. And I don't think she died in vain. There *is* a new consciousness around here. People are more committed to her project, and I think they are feeling better about it. They knew it wasn't right to keep destroying the forest like that. But they didn't know what to do about it.

"She had lots of beautiful qualities. You have to admire her, a missionary who goes the extra mile, goes to the toughest of places and starts to construct something completely different. But sometimes she was hard to take. That obstinacy of hers—it was as if her people were the only people who mattered, and everyone was expected to pitch in and help.

"But she did help me understand about the earth. About the whole ecosystem. And about new ways of caring for the earth. She helped people to see that. She wanted them to have a new vision of Amazônia, of the forest, of the forest people and how to work the land. Not destroying everything but creating a new relationship with nature. And creating a system that is a little more just. People understood that. That's why they wept when she died."

Many of the settlers were so desperate for land that even if they thought that Dorothy's ideas were unrealistic, they were happy to sign up for a plot of land on one of the two PDS projects. These projects had been designated in 1997, on land that had been declared unproductive and therefore eligible for land reform. But Dorothy knew that the land titles were disputed and took care to ask INCRA to check whether the area really had been cleared for the settlers to move in. Nobody imagined that it would take INCRA so long to reply, and the settlers grew tired of waiting and took matters into their own hands.

In January 1998, fifty families moved together onto an area of unused land on one of the interior roads on PDS Esperança. It was the beginning of the rainy season and they were already late for planting, so they set to work with a will. But it didn't take long for their presence to be noticed. Policemen and armed "security guards" visited the houses, informed the occupants that they were invaders, and told them that they must leave immediately. But on this occasion the people refused to be intimidated. Over Holy Week, Dorothy moved in to encourage their resistance, and she also arranged for a lawyer to intervene in their case. For the time being the families were able to stay on the land.

Later that year the settlers sent a delegation to the Pastoral Lands Commission and the Farm Workers' Union in Anapu to ask for technical assistance and moral support. In February

1999, the first public meeting was held in Anapu to discuss the question of the PDS. It was at this point that the settlers heard that the land was being claimed by a man named Genibaldo.

In one of Dot's letters from this time, she comments on how difficult the situation was, since SUDAM was financing large-scale projects on land that had been designated by INCRA for settlement. Litigation was virtually impossible, since the nearest courthouse was many miles away in Pacajá, and during the rainy season—January to June—the Transamazônica was often impassable. The settlers consoled themselves with the thought that if they could not get out, neither could anyone get in—until the day in May 1999 when Dani Gutzeit, Charles Storch, and Libério arrived by plane to say that they had taken over the land from Genibaldo and were setting up a SUDAM-financed project on lot 126. The settlers told the men that they would fight for their land and would sooner see them in court than negotiate.

Over the next few weeks Dani returned three times, offering the settlers money and jobs and attempting to negotiate, but, supported by their lawyer, the families stayed firm and started to prepare the land for planting. By November things had turned nasty. Dani reappeared with fifty armed men to expel the settlers. Shots were exchanged, and many of the settlers abandoned their plots. The authorities did nothing. Two weeks later the people moved back onto the land, but Dani filled the forest with gunmen, and many of the settlers left once again. Of the original fifty families, only twelve remained. In March 2000, Dani went in one more time and destroyed their houses, throwing quick-growing grass seed on their fields, which rendered them useless for cultivation, and leaving gunmen in charge.

Dani was later denounced by the public prosecutor's office for having swindled SUDAM out of 9 million reais, out of the 12 million he had received to set up productive enterprises in Altamira. The prosecutor's office stated that the whole process of SUDAM financing had been fraudulent from top to bottom, and implicated a total of fifty-eight people as members of the so-called SUDAM mafia. Dani testified that in order to obtain financing, he was obliged to pay a large bribe to Lionel Barbalho, brother of Jader Barbalho, a former governor and state senator who was later removed from his position but never suffered any serious punishment. Dani was later arrested by the federal police but was granted habeas corpus, at which point he took advantage of his dual nationality to settle in Switzerland.

In March 2001 a further meeting was held in Anapu to discuss the PDS. Technicians explained that this project involved a new style of farming. Traditional methods of slash and burn

would be replaced by planting in the forest itself, taking advantage of the shade, conserving the soil, and planting a greater variety of crops.

On March 12, 2002, thirty-one people reoccupied the land that they had settled in 1998 and that had subsequently been disputed by Dani Gutzeit. Fortunately, they took the precaution of getting confirmation from INCRA that the land was available for settlement. Three days later, five policemen showed up, but the settlers had their documents in order and were already building their houses and dividing up the land. Encouraged by their example, other families moved onto neighboring plots, and in the absence of official demarcation, they marked out their own boundaries.

Gunmen working for Luis Ungaratti and Marcos Oliveira, known as Marquinhos, then appeared on PDS Esperança and drove out a hundred families. Marquinhos set up a private settlement scheme on the land and selected 15,000 acres for local investors. The settlers appealed to INCRA, and on July 2, 2002, the agricultural ombudsman came to Anapu, together with some INCRA staff from Belém. The chief of INCRA from Altamira, Hugo Picança, promised to revalidate the settlers' claims.

The battle dragged on. In August 2002, visiting officials from the environmental protection agency IBAMA were frightened off by gunmen. Some of the settlers' lots were invaded and burned. Trees were illegally cut and timber was quietly shipped out along the river. INCRA remained supportive but did nothing. SUDAM financed several projects, and the settlers sent a delegation to Brasília to alert the federal government. Dot was accused of instigating land invasions, but the agricultural court in Marabá confirmed that the land in question was unproductive.

In November 2002 a meeting was held to officially create the two PDSes and approve the management plan. A photograph shows Dot in a white T-shirt, shoulders drooping but face defiant. She celebrated Christmas with the settlers on Esperança and they threw a party, complete with Santa Claus. The mayor promised them a road at kilometer 120 to improve access to the PDSes, but he failed to deliver, so in January 2003 they hired a tractor and built it themselves. On January 18 the settlers on Esperança held the founding meeting of their association, and three days later the settlers on Virola Jatobá followed suit.

Not all the potential settlers were in favor of the PDSes, however. A petition was sent to INCRA repudiating the idea, and documents urging people to reject it appeared throughout the area. They explained that on the PDSes, settlers would have no title to the land and no autonomy. They claimed that there was nothing to extract from the areas designated for extractive use, pointed out that no studies had been made to verify whether the land would be sustainable, stated that there had been no public consultation and that INCRA had never yet succeeded in setting up a workable project, and added that the project was headed by a foreigner who was probably at the service of international interests. That appeal to nationalism had never failed to work since the creation of the Transamazônica.

Geraldo was one of a small group that worked closely with Dorothy in her efforts to set up the PDSes. He arrived on the Transamazônica as a young boy, attended one of the first schools set up by Dorothy, studied to be an agricultural technician, and then returned to work on the project.

He describes their efforts to substitute a more sustainable way of farming for the culture of slash and burn. "That was the reason for the fruit factory," he says. "It was an attempt to help people stay on the land and make a decent living from it. Because they were starting to plant pasture, and that was awakening the interest of the ranchers. What happens is that once they've planted pasture, they can't grow their crops anymore and they have to sell up and move on.

"As you know, the factory was a long time in coming, but we finally got it operating in 2001, and we started by producing banana flour. We were working with 104 families to produce the bananas, but we couldn't get the marketing sorted out, and we ended up suspending operations in 2003. It was a tough job. It's far harder to restore the land than to preserve it in the first place. We were working with agroforestry, planting right in the forest instead of clearing the land. We managed to get seedlings, and we planted thousands of mahogany and other hardwoods.

"It was just about then that the government started talking about big projects like the Belo Monte dam, and that created huge pressure on the land and led to a lot of forest clearing. It was the time of the big migrations, when the population of the county was doubling from one year to the next. So we began to wonder whether we were knocking ourselves out to restore degraded areas on the one hand, while on the other there was all this devastation. And whether at the end of the day we were making any impact at all . . . Because the way things were going, the whole area was going to end up like one gigantic cattle ranch.

"So we stepped up our efforts to get the PDS up and running, and of course that infuriated the ranchers. There was a rush to clear the forest so that they could justify their presence on the land. Nobody could set foot on Esperança. It was full of land grabbers, and people were getting killed. Once when INCRA was doing a flyover to check on the forest clearing, they spotted a car on Fazenda Mercosul, and they later discovered that it was the headquarters for a gang of policemen from Marabá carrying out armed robbery and drug smuggling. They found out that businessmen from Anapu had been buying land right in the PDS and clearing the forest. The whole thing was a complete mess. And the more we were trying to help the settlers, the more enemies we were making."

On April 30, 2003, the mayor showed his hand. A motion of censure was passed by the town council of Anapu, declaring Dorothy Stang to be persona non grata. Sister Dorothy had been a threat to the peaceful and orderly citizens of Anapu, it said, ever since her arrival in the area, preaching outlandish ideas which were clearly aimed at the heroic pioneers who had braved the difficulties and dangers of the Transamazônica. Working with the federal police and government agencies, she sought to expel farmers from their lands and replace them with migrants who were submissive to her political maneuverings, which flew in the face of the progress that had been achieved in the area at such heavy cost. Furthermore, at a meeting of the town council held on April 26, 2003, the people of Anapu had unequivocally rejected the very idea of the PDS projects.

In an article published on June 4, Carlos Mendes describes the PDS as a "model of settlement which is capable of transforming disillusioned settlers who have lost hope of making a better life into agents of their own future. The main opposition comes from the loggers, traders, and large landowners, who

maintain that the PDSes are barriers to genuine progress, supported by the agents of large foreign powers who wish to take
over Amazônia." Yet Carlos saw these as daring and innovative
projects in a region where the tradition was fire and chain saw:
a new chance for the migrants who had been coming to Pará
over the previous ten years.

Despite increasing opposition, Dorothy battled on. In September and October, as a result of her persistence, a team of in-
spectors was brought in to check out the situation on the two
PDSes. The team consisted of representatives from IBAMA, the
military police, and the environmental agency, and they arrived
in a fleet of vehicles supported by a helicopter. Their first discov-
ery was a clandestine landing strip, marked with white painted
tires for night landings and takeoff. Large areas had been logged,
and a log landing had been cleared on the riverbank. They
found men at work using heavy machinery, unlicensed chain
saws, and firearms, and expired forestry licenses in the name of Zé
do Rádio, a well-known member of the group of illegal loggers
known as the mahogany mafia. The operation was closed down.

The team later discovered 53 million cubic feet of wood
stacked by the river, unlicensed clearing on land belonging to
both Délio Fernandes and the mayor, João Paraná, and unautho-
rized logging on land designated for the PDSes. They learned
that this had been carried out on the orders of Taradão, who was
also suspected of illegal trafficking in animals and fish. The in-
spectors returned with police reinforcements and heavy machinery and towed away the logging equipment.

It was becoming increasingly clear that if the settlers did not
occupy the land soon, there would be no forest left. In November, Geraldo moved onto Esperança with fifteen settlers and

built a small settlement of rough houses. INCRA surveyors started to work at the same time, but when confronted by armed men, they made a strategic withdrawal.

In June 2004, Dorothy was summoned to Belém to defend herself against accusations that she was arming and sheltering a group of settlers, and after two murders in the space of twenty-four hours the federal police were sent onto PDS Esperança. Four settlers were arrested and spent six months in jail. The mayor testified that the region was full of migrants looking for jobs, land, and riches, that the population of Anapu had tripled in three years, and that there were thirty-four logging firms in town. Anapu was one of the poorest counties in the state, with only one doctor, no television, and a precarious telephone system. "The fact is," he said, "that Anapu has been overtaken by bandits. This used to be a quiet little place, but over the past eighteen months the place has been overrun by criminals."

In October, Dot learned that a *pistoleiro* called Tufi had been hired by Yoaquim Petrola to kill her. The only reason he had not carried out his contract was that the terms had not been agreed upon.

In its annual report, *Rural Violence 2004,* the Pastoral Lands Commission published the names of 160 people throughout Brazil known to be threatened with death in connection with the land issue. Forty were from the state of Pará. Prices varied in accordance with the target: 5,000 reais for the leader of a settlement scheme, 8,000 for a dead *pistoleiro*, 10,000 for a union member, 15,000 for a town councillor, and 20,000 for a priest.

The top two targets were quoted as being worth substantially more, and number two, valued at 50,000 reais, was Sister Dorothy Stang.

FIFTEEN

THE ANGEL OF
THE AMAZON

So who was this woman, Dorothy, who was so rapidly getting herself into trouble with the local authorities and the large landowners? Who was loved and respected by many and known by some as the Angel and others as the Devil of the Transamazônica?

Clues can be found in the small house in Anapu that she shared with a changing cast of sisters, friends, and visitors. A simple wooden house painted faded aquamarine, it sits inside a picket fence. The front door leads into a small room which houses a collection of chairs strung with plastic, an elderly television set, and a statue of the Virgin Mary set around with candles. To the right is Sister Jane's cluttered room, where she keeps innumerable boxes full of documents and books. They overflow all the available space; a desktop computer is barely visible in one corner, and the only way she manages to sleep is by stringing a hammock.

The kitchen holds a table, stools, a bench under the window, a small gas stove, a collection of battered pots, and a sink— no fridge. Off the kitchen is a small bathroom with an electric shower and a cubbyhole with a flush toilet. A second bedroom is shared by two young Brazilian sisters, who sleep in hammocks and keep their possessions tidily arranged in the corners. Next door is Dorothy's room. The walls are painted, unexpectedly, in lilac; the window frames are green, and the cement floor is yellow. There is no glass in the windows, but unlike the rest of the house, this room has iron grilles over the windows. A table by the door holds a telephone and a fax machine. A hammock is stretched across one corner, beneath a wire used to hang the *padre*'s vestments. Somebody in the house must be caring for them and making sure they are ironed for Sunday mass.

The bed, with its sagging springs, is up against the wall, a mosquito net tidily knotted above it. A bookshelf is stacked with books, papers, and treasures: a black-and-white photograph of Henry and Edna, a Peruvian weaving, plastic flowers, a rosary, a crucifix. There is a crude clay bust of a woman praying, an Indian bell, a picture of the Annunciation, and a small velvet friendship pouch containing a pink heart made of translucent stone with the inscription "To you my friend I give my heart / To keep us close when we're apart / To carry ever by your side / In this small pouch my heart abides." Photos are stacked up next to books: Deepak Chopra, *Quantum Healing*; *Violence and Land Grabbing*; *The Religious Life*; Thomas Aquinas; *The Powers That*

Be. An umbrella leans against the wall next to a cloth bag of maps. There are papers everywhere, jammed into battered cardboard boxes, stuffed under the bed, and piled up against the wall.

Out back, tall mango trees shelter the outside shower and the table with its large plastic basins for clothes washing, and a cat's cradle of clotheslines is strung haphazardly across the yard. A shack overflowing with more clutter—boxes, bundles, a rusty bike—serves as a storage space and emergency shelter where people can hang their hammocks. A wooden gate leads to the church and beyond it to the parish hall, named for Padre Josimo, murdered during the land conflicts in Goiás twenty years ago. It has a cement floor, a little kitchen, two ancient freezers, and a sheltered outdoor area. Beyond it a little house is being used as an improvised barracks for the Jungle Battalion, sent to maintain law and order. Young soldiers in flak jackets patrol the dusty street.

Beyond the sisters' house lies the house of the *padres*. A large back veranda with two sinks and a water cooler provides a pleasant meeting space, although as night falls mosquitoes buzz round the potted plants which someone has placed along the top of the wall. During the day, when the two fierce watchdogs are caged, little boys steal in to pick the star and acerola fruit from the *padres'* garden, but after dark the dogs roam free and nobody stirs.

Padre Amaro is the parish priest; he is in his late thirties and is already running to fat—easy to do in this enervating climate, where it's hard to take exercise and the diet is starchy. Padre Amaro likes to wear Afro hats and models himself on the black martyr Padre Josimo. Like Josimo, his name figures prominently on the death lists in these parts, and the prelacy tries to ensure that he never travels alone. Once when he was in the backcountry he took a ride from a stranger who told him he was looking for "that terrorist black priest." Amaro stayed quiet, but when he reached his destination, the villagers ran up to him exclaiming, "Wherever have you been? We were worried about you, *padre*."

"Dorothy?" His eyes fill with tears. "I met her in '89. I was a seminarian in Belém and she paid for my group to come to Nazaré. Paid out of her own pocket. And what struck me was her simplicity. It was Farmers' Day, and there she was, up at six-thirty getting everything ready . . .

"Everyone talked about Dorothy. Dorothy was a myth, Dorothy was a witch, Dorothy was a saint, Dorothy was a devil, and I remember thinking, Whatever is going on here?

"She respected the church—oh, yes. But she was always Dorothy, uniquely Dorothy, Dorothy who was never afraid to speak up wherever she found herself. She didn't change her tune in front of the bishop or anyone else. She always stuck to her position. Always looked for the good in people. She used to say that however bad a person was, there was always a little good hidden away somewhere."

People who knew her well agree that Dorothy's life revolved around God, the people, and the land. She wasn't a nunnish kind of nun, and she didn't stuff religion down your throat. But she had a deep faith that her God would see her through. Nelda, the Brazilian sister who was with her during her last days, once asked Dorothy how she prayed. Dorothy smiled at her. "Nelda," she said, "I light a candle and I look at Jesus carrying his cross and I ask for the strength to carry the suffering of the people."

"She was a fighter," says Alci, a former postulant, who now helps to coordinate the Dorothy Committee, formed to carry on Dorothy's work. "And at the same time she was very calm. I think her personality was more disturbing than if she had been one of those firebrands always making public speeches. And determined? I remember all those visits that she paid to the government departments. They were always very polite: 'Good morning, Sister Dorothy, how are you, what can we do for you today?' But they'd make her wait for hours on end. She'd never lose her temper. I think she understood their game. She'd just wait there patiently looking through those papers of hers.

"I remember once she went off to see the president of INCRA and he refused to see her. She said she wasn't leaving until she had seen him. He wouldn't see her and she wouldn't leave. At the end of the day, everybody left the building, and she spent the night there. The security guard let her sleep on the sofa. None of us had any idea where she was, and we were out of our minds with worry. We knew they were out to get her, you see. It was the Pastoral Lands Commission lawyer Jerônimo who found her, at seven in the morning. Sitting there cool as a cucumber, drinking coffee and waiting for the president to arrive. She was smart, all right. But what was most impressive was her bond with the people."

Everyone agrees on that. "They trusted her utterly," Alci continues. "Because she was for them, body and soul. She'd travel for miles to go and visit them, hitching a ride if she could, otherwise going in on foot. She'd arrive covered with dust, with mud all over her shoes, baggy shorts, an Amazônia T-shirt, a baseball cap on her head and a pack on her back."

"She never stopped believing that the people she was

working with were the right people," says Rita, from the university. Dorothy once told Sister Liz, "I have to be with these people. If it means my life, I want to give my life."

"All she wanted was to see the people happy," Sister Maria says. "Happily settled on the land. She wanted them to live lives of dignity. She wanted to share her love of the earth—Mother Earth, who sustains us."

Just as she was welcomed into the poorest houses, she made a point of keeping an open door and a space at her own table. "Our community living in Anapu is family-based," she wrote. "We receive warmly whoever comes and attend to whatever needs they bring with them. Sometimes they come from our rural area to sit down at our community table, sometimes we put them up in hammocks so they can stay the night. We stay in their houses, so it's natural that they come to ours."

It drove Padre Nello wild. "You'd go to her house and there was never room to swing a cat," he remembers, laughing. "It would be packed with people. And she'd look at you with those blue eyes of hers and say, 'I've got to look after my people.' "

Dorothy regarded it as part of her mission. "Living, eating and drinking, sharing with these our people constantly challenges us to do all we can to help bring about change," she wrote, recalling her call to work with the poorest of the poor and going on to say that if she was truly to live the gospel of

Notre Dame, her conscience demanded that she take her stand wholeheartedly with her people. And one of her main concerns was with the women and children. Antonia, an activist from Altamira, says that without Dorothy, the women of the region might never have found their voice. Nivalda agrees. "Her real mission was with women," she declares. "Women and children. She wanted them to be free and equal and able to run their own lives. Now all you hear about is Dorothy the martyr for the forest, Dorothy saying you mustn't ever cut a tree. But it wasn't that. She wanted people to look after the earth just like they look after their own children. She felt that women would understand that."

Not that she didn't know how to enjoy herself. When she went to the States, she liked nothing better than watching a football game with a cold beer in hand, and in Brazil she enjoyed a *caipirinha*, a potent combination of fresh limes, sugar, and cane spirit. She adored ice cream, had a weakness for crunchy peanut butter, and was famous for her pancakes— although toward the end, most people agree, they were getting a little indigestible on account of her passion for natural ingredients. She loved to swim in the river, jump on the back of a dirt bike and head off into the forest, dance the *forró*, put on her yellow sunflower dress and go to a party. She decorated her own T-shirts and loved to paint pictures, and once she painted brilliant flowers over some bleach stains on one of Becky's skirts.

She loved being around people. She was a born educator who empowered people to take responsibility for their own lives, a grassroots organizer, and a creative thinker. She inspired people to dream, to plan, and to test their limits, and if they didn't always succeed, she helped them try again. Maria describes her as a natural leader, and points out that even in a macho society, the men admired her greatly. They listened to what she said, accepted many of her ideas, and even persuaded her to change some of her opinions. Gabriel from the union clashed with her over the question of political involvement, saying that all the schools and health posts in the world couldn't be built without funds and that the politicians held the purse strings. Dorothy listened politely and then gave a big laugh and told him he was right. But when Dorothy told the settlers that they shouldn't take up arms, they paid no attention.

Some called her smart and savvy; others called her ingenuous. She always believed in people and trusted them, perhaps further than she should have. She was living in dangerous times and a dangerous place, and when it came to protecting their lands and their livelihoods in a situation where they could rely on nobody except themselves, the settlers weren't about to settle for passive resistance. And Dorothy was breaking taboos by denouncing the land grabbers by name. As a woman and a foreigner, she was treading on dangerous ground.

Nobody could remain indifferent to Dorothy. To Felício, the federal prosecutor who was struggling in the public prosecutor's office to change the culture of impunity, it was love at first sight. One of the settlers described what he felt when Dorothy died: "Like a river without water, like a forest without trees." Alci speaks of her contagious energy, which touched everyone. Her oldest friend, Joan, writes, "We all know the movement of God in Sister Dorothy's life. Her love of God and of her people, her reverence for the forest and the animal and bird life the forest nourishes, took such a hold on her that her sole concern was the safety of the people and the preservation of the forest."

Her understanding of nature dated back to her childhood, to the days when she used to work in the vegetable garden at Markey Road and go for walks with her father in search of wild mushrooms. When she moved to Pará, she focused on the land in terms of its ability to nourish life for migrant families. But after she had witnessed the devastating effects of slash-and-burn agriculture and seen how first the forest and then the earth itself had been destroyed, she came to a new understanding of how people should live in the forest. She studied creation spirituality, she talked to hundreds of environmentalists at the Earth Summit, and she grieved over the senseless devastation of the greatest forest on earth and the legacy of human suffering left in its wake. And here she clashed with the loggers and ranchers, who saw themselves as bold pioneers creating wealth and employment.

"She came up against a lot of opposition and a lot of criticism," says Becky. "From the ranchers and the authorities, of course. But also from the bishop, the priests, and the sisters. It hurt. And she had a hard time with that. With criticism from the church and from men. She needed approval from men. I guess it came from her relationship with her father. She needed approval, and it hurt her when she didn't get it."

After her death, a magazine called *Hoje,* published by the

large landowners in Altamira, described her as a troublemaker who had led a land invasion back in 1970 and had then come to Anapu, where she appeared on the scene as a martyr in defense of the indefensible PDSes. But the magazine's editors were concerned too over all the unknown factors associated with her death. "Careful analysis reveals a high-level conspiracy, with the immaculate nun serving as a sacrificial lamb whose sacred blood could justify the spurious interests of the Workers' Party, the Catholic Church, and foreign NGOs," the writer states, adding that the federal government had failed its citizens by not paying due attention to what Dorothy was doing in terms of the land situation. Since she had taken it upon herself to do the job of the government agencies IBAMA and INCRA, the outcome was written in the stars. She even refused police protection. "Was this," the writer speculates, "because she was defending legitimate interests? Or was she afraid of being watched by the police lest they discover what was really behind this ecclesiastical murder?"

The union of loggers accused her of "instigating conflict in the region for the past twenty years and establishing an extractive project without a feasibility study," as well as "opening the way to biopiracy, since she works for a North American organization."

But despite any internal disagreements, the Sisters of Notre Dame presented a united front in defense of Dorothy. "She was a strong woman," says her best friend, Joan, smiling as she adds, "but sometimes very obstinate. She had a soft voice that echoed through the halls of government offices and bounced off the giant trees of the forests, the same soft voice that could soothe an aching heart and assure someone that God loved them. Dot had a mind that could understand the laws of land reform, the intricacies of sustainable farming, the impact of the destruction of the forest on the world now and in the future, and the hope and conviction that one voice could make a difference."

Marlene de Nardo, who taught Dot creation spirituality, adds that her smile "seemed to speak to her incredible hope and belief that if you or I knew about this problem, we would all surely do something to change it. Dot's smiling countenance could be disturbing and challenging, and rightly so. How does one respond to such conviction, to radical radiance and transparency?" She also refers to Dot's "single-mindedness and utter simplicity," which some referred to as naiveté, and points out that it was this quality of single-mindedness that made her intrepid.

Dot's eldest sister, Mary, recalls the last time they saw each other, in the summer of 2004. Dot was showing her sister articles clipped from the papers accusing her of selling ammunition. Mary maintains that Dot never had the money for guns and never even knew how to handle one. Dot's second sister, Norma, hadn't seen her since 1999, but they spoke periodically on the phone. "My sister was tough," she declares. "Otherwise she wouldn't have survived so many years and accomplished what she did. She died doing what she loved. How many people in life get that?" Norma's twin, Maggie, says that Dot's people are devastated. "They didn't want a martyr, they wanted her alive." David points out that "she was not by any means a sweetly pious nun who had retreated to a life of prayer and contemplation. She was tough, smart, and intensely political. It was precisely her fervent work on behalf of the poor that got her killed. None of this little nun bit. She was like a Mack truck."

One way to find out about Dorothy is to look at her letters to her many friends and her large family. They take the form of photo journals recounting day-to-day events, written in her slanting handwriting on A4 paper. The mood is nearly always upbeat, minimizing the difficulties and dangers she faced.

Talking to Bobby in 2003, in reply to a request for a personal reflection on life in Brazil, she wrote, "I have learned that faith sustains you. And I have also learned that three things are difficult. 1) as a woman to be taken seriously in the struggle for land reform, 2) to stay faithful to believing that these small groups of poor farmers will prevail in organizing and carrying their own agenda forward, and 3) to have the courage to give your life in the struggle for change."

In an article for *Outside* magazine in 2003, Dorothy acknowledged the danger but laughed it off, saying, "The logging companies work with a threat logic. They elaborate a list of leaders and then a second movement appears to eliminate those people. If I catch a stray bullet, we'll know exactly who did it."

But later on, as if to reassure herself, she said, "They'll never have the courage to kill an old woman like me."

SIXTEEN

A DEATH FORETOLD

By now Dorothy had lived long enough in Latin America to know the ritual of the death foretold: the gossip on the streetcorners, the hints, the vague threats; attempts to isolate and criminalize the victim; accusations of flying in the face of progress, of encouraging armed invasion, of providing food and guns to the settlers. The town council of Anapu had declared her persona non grata, thereby ensuring that most of the population, which depended in one way or another on the employment and perks provided by the county, would not dare to support her. The word went around that she was interfering in government business, that she was in over her head, that she wasn't behaving like a proper nun.

People declared that they didn't want anything to do with the PDSes, and some of them called for her expulsion.

"She knew, of course," said one of the sisters. "And as time went by she was getting a little discouraged." On Dot's last visit to Ohio, in the summer of 2004, Liz remarked that "in spite of her cheerfulness, she seemed to have the whole weight of the Amazon rain forest on her shoulders." Her old friend Joan said that for the first time Dot seemed discouraged. "Her shoulders drooped, and she told me, 'We're losing the battle.'" Sister Virginia said to her, "I can't stand to think you'll go back to Brazil, because it's not a question of if you'll be assassinated but when."

The sisters were very concerned about her, and even discussed the possibility of her leaving Brazil for a while. But of course she didn't want to. In public she put a brave face on it, saying, "Who would kill an old nun like me?" and she told the sisters, "I can't worry about the danger. It's the people who are important."

But the risks were very apparent to her siblings David and Maggie when they visited her, on the spur of the moment, in December 2004 and learned of the price on her head. "Everywhere we went, people told her to be careful," remembers David. "People were hugging each other as if it were the last time." She kept talking about the way people were destroying the forest and nobody was doing anything to stop it. "I think she felt a new sense of urgency."

Shortly after that, Dot's Brazilian citizenship came through. Perhaps she thought it would protect her.

Her faith in the authorities led her to make repeated denunciations of the land grabbers and loggers, thereby building herself a powerful collection of enemies: Luis Ungaratti, Délio

Fernandes, Marcos Oliveira, Yoaquim Petrola, Taradão, and perhaps even bigger fish, like the Barbalho family. They owned one of the two newspapers in Belém, they controlled the industrial town of Ananindeua, and they had fingers in many pies.

Again and again Dorothy went to the authorities with names and dates, denouncing land grabbing and illegal logging to INCRA, IBAMA, the state and federal police, and the public prosecutor's office. She wrote to the state secretary for social welfare describing the climate in Anapu as one of war, and as a result of her denunciations, some of the loggers were fined heavily.

She was summoned by the police to testify in the case of Fazenda Rio Anapu. The settlers accused a band of armed gunmen of trying to expel them from their land, while Yoaquim Petrola de Melo, who also claimed to be the owner of Fazenda Manduacari, stated that his property had been invaded by Sister Dorothy's men. In the ensuing shootout, his employee Moises Andrade had been killed, and this death had unleashed a chain of accusations against Sister Dorothy. She was supporting the invasion. She had supplied food to the invaders. She was running guns. She would have to answer to this before a court of law.

She was stoutly defended by her friends and supporters. Public prosecutor Felício sent a note to the state secretary for social welfare asking that Dorothy be given police protection. The sisters in Ohio wrote a letter of support declaring that the accusations against her were absurd and false and that she had never encouraged violence. In June 2004 she was awarded the title of Honorary Citizen of Pará, and six months later she received the Humanitarian of the Year Award from the Brazilian Bar Association.

"I'm threatened with death by the ranchers and the land grabbers," she reported. "They had the nerve to threaten me and demand my expulsion from Anapu. And all because I cry out for justice."

Meanwhile, the situation on Esperança was deteriorating by the day. The settlers continued to live in a state of terror. Houses were burned, fields were ruined, and some of the families gave up and left. Dorothy had her back to the wall, but she battled on, sending a stream of protests to local, state, and federal authorities. The state governor, Simão Jatene, was informed of the explosive situation in Anapu, but he neither replied to the letter nor acknowledged it. Heedless of her safety, Dorothy continued to name names. One of them was Bida, who had recently arrived on Esperança, claiming to be the owner of several lots right inside the PDS, which he said he had bought from Taradão. It was his henchman, Tato, who had been responsible for burning Luis's *barraca*. Dorothy gave the federal secretary for human rights a list of the people in Anapu known to be marked for death: Padre Amaro, Chiquinho from the union, Gabriel, and Dorothy herself.

At the same time, among a small circle of people in Altamira the word was going around that something needed to done about Dorothy. Nobody knows exactly who belonged to the group that got together one night in January 2005 in a hotel in Altamira to discuss the matter. Nobody knows who attended that meeting, or if they know, they aren't saying. But names are suggested quietly, in a roundabout fashion. Names like Luis dos Reis Carvalho, the mayor of Anapu. The mayor of Porto de Moz. Délio Fernandes, Luis Ungaratti, Yoaquim Petrola, Taradão, Bida. No one knows for sure, but the word got out on the street. Someone heard someone talking in the bar. That woman's days were numbered.

Undaunted, Dorothy delivered a letter to the Pará civil police chief, Luis Fernandes, stating that Bida and Tato were threatening the settlers on Esperança, and later that day she attended the launching of the National Witness Protection Program and spoke with the federal secretary for human rights, Nilmário Miranda.

Dorothy had lived through dangerous moments before. She'd hidden out in the forest on several occasions, and once she'd taken refuge behind a truck when she ran into an ambush. But on the weekend that someone planned to kill her, she wasn't in Anapu. It was Carnival, and she was in Belém.

She was staying with the sisters in their hot little wooden house in Guamá, a very poor area of town. In Belém they call these areas *baixadas*, but in the other towns in Brazil they are known as *favelas*. You enter off a busy road that leads out of town, heading for the banks of the River Guamá and the campus of the Federal University. The sidewalks are all broken up, and open drains run alongside the road. When it rains the whole area is underwater, and although people swear there's no malaria, it's a good place to catch dengue fever.

The nuns have painted their house and planted flowers outside. A sign propped up in the flowerbed says, PLEASE DON'T THROW GARBAGE, but nobody pays any attention. The streets are full of blowing plastic bags, rotting fruit, dog turds, and worse, and the noise never stops: children crying; people talking, shouting, laughing, and arguing, always at full volume; cars and motorbikes roaring through; sometimes gunshots. Drugs are dealt on the corner, beggars stop at the sisters' window and ask for a little coffee or a bite to eat, and children wave as they pass on their way to school.

The kitchen table is covered with a clear plastic cloth, and there's a poster on the door demanding *Land Reform Now!* Hand-lettered signs on the walls say, WELCOME! YOU ARE SPECIAL TO US. HOW GOOD IS THE GOOD GOD! There's a small gas stove, a cheap wooden cupboard painted blue, an ancient refrigerator, and a shelf with mugs hanging underneath. A small space behind the sink holds an elderly washing machine, which isn't used very often, and leads to the yard, where two concrete sinks are used for clothes washing and clothes are dried on a series of lines strung about the place. The room that leads off the garden has a couple of school desks, a shelf of books, and several hammock hooks, and a narrow spiral staircase leads upstairs to the chapel and a small bedroom with three narrow beds in a row. Back in the main house, a steep wooden staircase leads up to two small bedrooms and an office which houses a computer with sticky keys, and on the other side of the staircase a sitting room and a small cubbyhole for the telephone. On hot afternoons the young sisters curl up on the cement floor of the upstairs chapel with all the windows open to snatch a quick siesta.

It was Mary Cohen, a lawyer from the Brazilian Bar Association, who recommended Dorothy for the Humanitarian of the Year Award in December 2004, and she had immediately fallen under Dorothy's spell. When Dorothy was in Belém, Mary offered her any legal advice or help she might need. That last week the two spent a whole day working on Dorothy's documents, and Mary pressed her to spend the weekend. But Dot said she couldn't. She said that her people were waiting for her.

She stopped by at the house of her friend Marga for lunch. Marga gave her a whole pile of newspapers and magazines to take to the sisters, and she listened to Dorothy's stories and told her that she ought to go talk to the bishop. He ought to know what was going on. "She looked at me with those blue eyes of hers," said Marga, "and she said, 'Marga, do you think he doesn't know? He watches the news, he reads the papers—he knows. He must have his reasons for not doing anything.' Of course she didn't want to talk to the bishop in case he told her to leave. She would have had to obey. Or maybe not."

Padre Nello remembers that Dorothy came staggering in with a huge pile of papers to copy in the office of the Indigenous Missionary Council. "She had so much to do and she was in such a state that she started getting things wrong." He smiles. "I said to her, 'Dorothy, why don't we take a lunch break?' And she said, 'I can't possibly do that. I haven't the time.' But when we said, 'OK, how about a little drink instead?' she said, 'Now that's a different story. I could manage that all right.'"

"It was the weekend of Carnival," says Sister Julia. "I remember seeing her sitting on her bed, very thoughtful. I said to her, 'Dorothy, are you OK? Why don't you stay on for a few days? What's the point of going back now? It's not as if anything will happen over Carnival.'

"Well, she didn't say anything for a minute, and then she looked up at me and said she had to go back for a meeting. That wretched meeting. They were dividing up the land and they were arguing about it. I think, myself, she was remembering those men saying to her, 'Woman, the day you set foot on our land, we'll kill you.' That's what I think. She never said anything. But I think she knew. I think she knew that death was near."

SEVENTEEN

FEBRUARY 11, 2005

The Toyota plowed to a halt outside the police station, and Dorothy pushed the door open. "Good morning," she called out cheerfully. "We're just heading off to Esperança. Are you guys ready?"

"Good morning, Sister Dorothy," said the sergeant. "Just a minute—let me check with the boss." He disappeared out back, and there was a pause. Dorothy sighed. Just a minute, just a minute. How many minutes, hours, weeks, and months had she spent waiting? Waiting for other people to do their job? And how many times had she been refused? She knew deep down that she couldn't trust the local police chief. But maybe, just maybe this time . . . Dear

God, let them say yes, she begged. Just this once let them say yes.

She stared out the window. It was raining steadily, and she knew that the road would be bad. She thought of Padre Amaro in Altamira with Felício. They were going to the grand opening of the first extractive reserve in the area, in the small town of Porto de Moz on the Xingu River. All sorts of dignitaries would be present, including the federal environment minister, and it would be a great day in the struggle for sustainability. There'd been a lot of local opposition to the reserve, stirred up by the mayor of Porto de Moz. He had been heard to declare that extractive reserves created no employment, paid no taxes, and were a backward model of development. Furthermore, if that Sister Dorothy attempted to interfere in the internal affairs of his county, he knew how to take care of her . . .

Padre Amaro had done his best to persuade Dorothy to go with them, but she had been adamant. She had promised to hold a meeting on Esperança, and she couldn't let the settlers down. Beside, she had good news for them. INCRA had reaffirmed that their documents were in order. As for the gunmen who'd been going around burning houses, she was sure she could convince them to leave the settlers in peace. It wasn't as if they stood to gain anything themselves; they were simply working for Tato and Bida and the others. And if she happened to run into either of those two, she would have the backing of the police. The police chief in Belém had given his word.

The minutes dragged on, and Dorothy was left alone.

The door opened and the sergeant appeared. "I'm sorry, Sister Dorothy," he began, and Dorothy knew immediately what he was going to say. For a second she couldn't breathe. So they were not going to help her after all. Through a wave of dizziness she heard the sergeant's voice. There was going to be a demonstration in town next day; they were having a problem with transport. The police chief was extremely sorry . . .

Dorothy took a deep breath. They were on their own. "Thank you, sergeant." Her voice was hardly above a whisper as she turned to leave. God give me strength, God give me strength, she thought as she walked stiffly back to the waiting car. Ivan looked at her questioningly, and she shook her head. "No luck," she told him. "They say they don't have a car."

Dorothy settled back into her seat and attempted to still her whirling thoughts. The police had consistently refused them protection, so why had she imagined that this time things might be different? This business of the PDS had been a battle from the start, but surely the authorities could see now that things were turning nasty? And the worst was that it was nobody's fault. Not really. The root cause was the question of land titling, a confusion that dated back thirty years. When INCRA scheduled the land for settlement, they didn't take notice of the fact that some of the original concessions had never been canceled. Things had started coming to a head in January, when Tato had turned up on lot 55 announcing that he had bought three plots of land from his old friend Bida, who had bought them from Taradão. When Tato went in to inspect them, he discovered that some guy called Luis had put up a house right on his property. Worse still, the settlers were clearing his land. But nobody was living in the house, so he'd sent a couple of his men to take it over, and they'd turned it into a storage space for sacks of grass seed and fertilizer. Tato wanted to get his pasture planted as soon as possible, while the rains were good.

His men lost no time in telling the settlers that they were going to have to move off the land, and the families on Esperança didn't know quite how to react. True, there had been some ugly incidents. But things were different now. Sister Dorothy had told them it would be all right, because Dr. Roberto Kiehl was coming to sort things out. He was the president of INCRA, and he was coming all the way from Brasília just to see them. Weary of violence, the settlers took Dorothy at her word, and when she asked them to find a suitable spot to hold the meeting, they answered that the only house big enough was the one that Luis had built. They knew that there were gunmen living there, so they took as many men as they could raise, and they told Tato's men that they were going to have to clear the house for the meeting. Tato didn't like that one bit, but he couldn't do anything to stop them, and things got even worse when Luis arrived with his large family and moved in. Tato's men had made a rough plastic shelter right next door, and he took himself off there for the night. But he wasn't happy about it.

After that Luis and his family lived uneasily alongside Tato's men, Rayfran, Eduardo, and Curupira, until the day that Tato arrived and told him that enough was enough; he was going to have to get out of the house. In desperation, Luis told Tato that he had no place to go, that the courts were looking into the question of the land ownership, and that he'd been told by INCRA that he could move there. But, he added quickly, if the courts judged against him, he would leave quietly. If they judged in his favor, he would stay. Faced with such an unexpected show of spirit, Tato retreated, but some days later he was back, and this time he told Luis that if he didn't get out, he would burn his house down.

Dorothy was horrified when she heard that Tato had carried out his threat, and ran immediately to the police station in Anapu to register a complaint. A few days later she took Luis to Belém to testify to the federal police and to the federal secretary for human rights, adding that Tato's men were spreading grass seed on the settlers' fields, which would mean that they couldn't grow any crops.

Dorothy had lots of friends and supporters in Belém, and when she returned to Anapu on Monday, February 7, right at the height of Carnival, she was carrying the documents that INCRA had given her supporting the settlers' claim to be on the land. Her friends in Belém had begged her to stay on for a few days; it was the holiday season, and nothing would happen for the rest of the week. But out on Esperança people didn't stop for Carnival, and Dorothy was anxious to get home and prepare for the settlers' meeting at the weekend.

By the time the Toyota arrived on Esperança, it was long past lunchtime, and their first stop was at the house of Dona Maria to drop off the rice and beans that were to feed the community over the weekend. Maria insisted on giving them a glass of coffee and some fried manioc after their journey, and Dorothy excitedly told her that she had good news for the settlers and that she would tell them all about it at the meeting. They'd have the whole weekend to discuss it. She wanted to hear everyone's story, because they were going to build a joint future together and they'd need to know where they had come from.

They picked up Maria and her family and drove on down to Manoel's house, where the meeting was to be held. A small crowd had gathered there already, and Dorothy had a word for each one. "Do you know what I'd like to do before we start?" she said. "I'd like to go see the site of the community center."

There was a moment's pause, and then several people spoke at once.

"Well?" asked Dorothy with a smile. "Who wants to come and show me?"

"Listen to me, Sister Dorothy." Maria's voice rose above the others. "You're not to go there, do you hear me? It isn't safe. Tato's had a bunch of men working up there for the past few days, and we can't figure out what he's up to. But whatever it is, he's up to no good. And we're doing our best to stay out of his way."

Geraldo frowned. "If that's the case," he said, "we'd best not go."

"Of course we'll go," said Dorothy decisively.

Everyone fell silent.

"Well," said Gabriel slowly, "just one or two of us, OK? There's no point in provoking them. I'll go with you."

"I'm coming," said Geraldo.

"Me too," Nelda heard herself say. It was the first time that she had been in the forest; she found the huge trees intimidating, and she felt safer close to the comforting presence of Sister Dorothy.

They climbed into the Toyota and drove past the blackened stumps that were all that remained of Luis's house, past the clearing where Rayfran and Eduardo had been throwing grass seed onto the settlers' fields, past the crude wooden shack belonging to Vicente, down the hill where a small track led off to Bida's farm, and steeply up the road to the future headquarters of PDS Esperança. As they picked their way carefully along the slippery path into the forest, they could hear the sound of chain saws. Nelda tensed. Through the trees she could make out some figures bent over a huge tree that had just been felled. One of them was sawing planks; another was splitting wood shingles with an ax. The other two were sitting on a log, smoking. She felt the hairs on the back of her neck standing on end. Dorothy walked ahead calmly, with Gabriel and Geraldo on either side of her.

"Good afternoon, my friends," she said. "What's going on here?"

"See for yourself," said one of the men shortly. "We're building a house."

"And whose house are you building?" inquired Dorothy, a slight edge to her voice.

"Mine," came the answer.

"I'm sorry," said Dorothy. "There must be some mistake. You can't build here. This land belongs to the PDS."

The four men were standing in a tight little group, and for a moment nobody said anything. "Yes," continued Dorothy hastily, "it belongs to the PDS. And we've come to hold a series of meetings over the weekend to explain the situation to everyone. There's been a lot of confusion, as you know, but thank God it's all sorted out now. The settlers can go ahead and start planting." She reached inside her cloth bag and pulled out an envelope. "These are the documents from INCRA, so everything is settled. In fact, we're just about to have the first meeting. Tato, why don't you come along too? You'd be most welcome."

Tato said nothing.

"Do come," said Nelda. "Then we can explain everything properly."

Tato ignored her and turned to the little old lady who was standing in his way. "Now listen here, Sister," he said levelly. "I have two things to say to you. First of all, I don't have any interest in your stupid little PDS. And second, I don't have to answer to anyone, anyone at all, about what I do on my land. Do you hear? Go ahead and call your federal police if you want. Fifty men won't get me out of here."

Dorothy looked up at him. "My son," she began in her soft voice, "get your men to pull up that grass that they've planted, because it's starting to germinate already. Go home and look after your family, and forget all this wickedness."

Tato narrowed his eyes. "Sister Dorothy," he said slowly and distinctly, "let me tell you something. If you insist on putting your men on my land, you won't be able to count the number of bodies that leave this place on a stretcher."

Gabriel stiffened. He knew that the men were armed and that Dorothy had overstepped the mark. It had become a personal issue between the two, and one that could easily be resolved—by four shots. He took Dorothy's arm, gripping it tighter than he meant to. "Come on, Dorothy," he told her. "We've got to get out of here. Now." The couple of hundred yards back to the road were the longest walk of his life, and every second he expected to hear the crack of a bullet.

Geraldo felt the sweat start in his armpits and smelled the rank smell of his own fear. As he turned, one of the gunmen stepped in front of him. "*Filho de puta!*" he taunted him. "Don't mess around with us."

Nelda was trembling so hard that she wondered if she could

walk. God have mercy, God have mercy, God have mercy, she thought, as she put one foot in front of the other and followed Dorothy's erect figure back to the road.

They climbed into the Toyota in complete silence. Tato's truck was parked nearby, and hardly had they set off before they heard the sound of his engine gunning along the road behind them.

When they reached Manoel's house, the settlers were already gathering for their meeting, and the word went around like wildfire. Some of them wanted to leave straightaway. They were terrified of Tato; hadn't he burned Luis's house out from under him? And Cícero's? And Zé's? That man would stop at nothing, and they weren't all going to sit around waiting to be killed.

Dorothy looked around at the anxious faces, and the muttering stopped. "Don't worry, people," she said. "No one will hurt us. They're just trying to frighten us off, that's all. There are more of us than them, and God is with us, right? Now let's sit down and plan this weekend. This meeting is very, very important, and we need to make sure that everyone comes. So when you go home tonight, make sure that you talk to your neighbors, you talk to everyone you meet, and tell them to be here tomorrow bright and early. Tell them we've got work to do."

The settlers said nothing, and Nelda could sense that they were nervous. And she knew that nervous men were hard to handle. She tightened her grip on her rosary beads: Holy Mary, Mother of God, pray for us sinners, now and at the hour of our death, now and at the hour of our death, now and at the hour of our death . . .

It was growing dark inside as rainclouds gathered for the afternoon storm. Nelda looked around the room at the men with their faces seamed by the sun, their callused hands resting on their knees, the women with the children on their laps, one young mother suckling her baby, two small boys playing with a kitten in the corner. There was a commotion in the doorway, and a young man came in. He was wearing a cowboy hat and jeans and smoking a cigarette. Nelda could see that he had a pistol stuffed in the waistband of his jeans. He surveyed the settlers, a faint smile on his lips. Dorothy looked steadily at him. She didn't know his face, but she could guess his profession. "What we want here," she said, raising her voice a little, "is peace. We want to live together in peace." The young man gave her a slight smile and walked out.

"This meeting," Dorothy continued, "will be to talk about the PDS. Now that we have the land, we need to figure out how we can work together. It's not just about lot 55. Yes, I know that's our chief concern. But that's all in the past. We're talking about the future. That's why it's so important that everyone comes. We've worked hard for this moment, and now we can all take a little time out together to dream. And we are especially lucky to have Genilson with us. He's a specialist in growing cocoa. He says conditions here are just right, and he's going to tell us all about it and how we can grow it. I'm sure there isn't a person here who doesn't love chocolate."

People began to relax a little, and the meeting wound on. A car drove past, and then they heard it return and stop outside. Nelda turned around just as Tato and his men walked up and stood right next to the door, talking loudly and laughing. The settlers did their best to ignore them, but the atmosphere in the room had suddenly become charged, and although there was much to discuss, one by one the settlers fell silent. Shortly after five Dorothy brought the meeting to a close, refusing Geraldo's suggestion that she return to Anapu with him, because there was far too much to do and she wanted to get started early in the morning.

"In that case, you'll come and sleep in my house," said Maria firmly.

"Oh, Maria," said Dorothy, "you know I'd love that. The others can stay with you. But I've just been invited to Vicente's. He wants to talk to me."

The settlers dispersed, their mood subdued, and Dorothy set off down the road with Nelda and Maria. It wasn't long before it started raining, a steady rain that soaked them to the skin. Not that it mattered in that climate, but Dorothy was carrying her precious documents in a cloth bag, so they ducked into Cícero's house to shelter. There wasn't much room to get out of the rain, since Cícero's house had been all but destroyed in a fire. Cícero had hidden out in the forest when he saw the gunmen coming, but later he had crept back and fixed up a plastic sheet over the little storeroom out back, which they hadn't bothered to burn. The three women huddled inside the storeroom, and seconds later they heard a car driving past.

After ten minutes or so the rain lifted a little and they set out once again. It was overcast and would soon be dark, and even though Dorothy carried her solar-powered lantern, they were anxious to be safely off the road before nightfall. But as fast as they walked, they couldn't escape the next shower, and just as they were approaching Vicente's house it started to rain in earnest.

Geraldo was heading back to Anapu and kicking himself for not having said something when Dorothy had announced she was going to spend the night with Vicente. He'd never been able to bring himself to trust the man, and he'd even discussed it with Dorothy. But she always thought the best of everyone. She used to tell Geraldo that there was a little spark of good in every single one of God's creatures, and when Geraldo argued that Vicente was always hanging out with Tato and his men and taking odd jobs with them, Dorothy laughed and told him not to be so hard on the poor man. It wasn't as if he had a thing in the world except his little daughter, so you couldn't wonder if he wanted to earn some money from time to time.

Geraldo had taken that to heart, and one day when he was passing he had stopped his motorbike and gone in to have a chat with Vicente. He'd asked him if he wanted a plot of land on the PDS or whether he preferred to work with Tato. Vicente had given a wry little smile and told him that yes, of course he'd like a plot of land. But he'd never yet met a settler who had offered him any work, and he had his daughter to think of. Geraldo laughed and said he understood perfectly, but they were hoping that the settlers could live well enough off their land that they wouldn't need to depend on the big landowners. But Geraldo still had his doubts about Vicente, and when he heard later on that Rayfran and Eduardo used to hang out in his house in the evenings, he felt sure that his instincts had been correct.

The settlers' houses were all built of saplings with grass roofs and dirt floors, yet even so they were clean and welcoming inside. But Vicente's house was one of the poorest, and he lived alone with his little daughter. He had draped black plastic sheeting roughly over the roof and walls to keep the rain out, but inside the house there was nothing but a clay stove in the corner, a rough table on which was placed a tray with three glasses and an earthenware pot of water, a couple of hammocks, and two stools. Nelda took one look at the little girl with her tangled hair and shy smile and went over and started talking to her. The rain was pounding hard on the roof. Maria and Dorothy went to stand by the fire, and Vicente busied himself heating a pan of water for coffee.

There was a noise outside, and Nelda looked up to see a couple of men approaching the house. "Hey, Vicente," one of them shouted, stamping the mud off his boots as he stepped out of the rain. "Having a party here, hey? Give us a drink of water, will ya? The stinking road is so frigging muddy it doesn't look like we'll get out of here in a hurry." Nelda shivered as she recognized Tato and Rayfran. Tato drew Vicente outside, and the two held a muffled conversation. Vicente called roughly to the girl and told her to bring some water for Tato. "He drank out of the same glass as I had," Nelda said later. "If only I'd known."

Maria waited for the two men to leave before looking out and announcing that they'd best be off. "What about those men?" asked Nelda nervously. "Never you mind about them," said Maria robustly. "They live the other way from us. Now let me tell you about that Rayfran. A bad lot if ever I saw one. I remember the day they burned Luis's house . . ." Nelda would rather have talked about anything other than this, but Maria was not to be deterred. "I took one look at their faces," she told her, marching along the slippery road, "and I ran over to my house, knelt down by my hammock, and I said six Hail Marys."

Dorothy could no longer sleep comfortably in a hammock,

since it made her back ache. But she carried a camping mattress, which she unrolled on the floor. She hung her solar lantern on a hook on the wall, propped her cloth bag in the corner, settled herself on one of the stools, and smiled at her host. "Now, Vicente," she said. "What was it that you wanted to talk to me about?"

EIGHTEEN

FEBRUARY 12, 2005

"Come on, Rayfran," Tato growled. "Let's get moving. If we stick around in this weather, we'll never get the frigging truck out of here."

He was looking forward to a night in town. There were supplies to be collected—food, gasoline, and a new chain for the saw. Always something. And a foul night for a drive. Just as well that Rayfran had changed the tire; the old one had been completely bald.

They climbed into the gray Ford truck and he accelerated hard up the hill, but halfway up the truck lost traction and skidded backward, until its back wheels were embedded in the deep mud by the side of the road. "Frigging truck," he muttered. "Frigging stupid truck.

Stupid thing can't even get up the road, for God's sake. Get out and give her a push. I don't fancy spending the night in this god-forsaken forest."

Rayfran took a drag on his cigarette and peered out into the blackness. At least the rain had eased off. "Put her in second," he told Tato, "and I'll give her a push. But she's so frigging heavy I doubt I can shift her." Tato revved the engine while Rayfran put his shoulder to the bodywork and leaned all his weight, but the truck didn't budge, and one of the back wheels dug itself deeper, spraying him with glutinous red mud. "Try again," urged Tato from the relative comfort of the cab, but this time the back of the truck slewed around, and if Rayfran hadn't jumped out of the way it would have knocked him over.

"Jesus Christ!" exclaimed Tato. "We'll just have to walk."

It was pitch black, the road was slippery, and there was a fine mist of rain, all of which combined to put Tato in a foul mood. He stomped along in silence for a few minutes, pondering. Things weren't looking good. Just when he thought he had taken care of those pesky settlers, they had popped up again and were going to spend the weekend talking about the land. It was all on account of that interfering old woman who called herself a nun. Encouraging people to invade his land. Telling them that INCRA said it was all right, that INCRA said they could move onto land that had been properly registered, that INCRA said he couldn't plant up his own fields. Who in the hell did she think she was, speaking for INCRA? Everyone knew that INCRA had never done anything to help anyone. They'd sent in a bunch of surveyors only a few weeks earlier, and what had happened to them? Didn't last more than a day. Said it was impossible for them to do their job.

And that Dorothy, running around as if she were the savior of the people. Encouraging land invasions. People even said she'd asked the police to protect her. But luckily they had more sense than to do that. They had a job to do and couldn't be wasting their time acting as bodyguards to an old lady.

Bodyguards to an old lady? What bodyguards? Wasn't she sleeping in Vicente's house tonight? Silly old fool, didn't she know whose side Vicente was on?

Tato stopped dead in his tracks. "Rayfran," he said, turning to his companion. "Rayfran, my boy. You're man enough to kill that old woman, aren't you?"

Rayfran's thoughts were far away. He was seeing himself on his own piece of land with his own cattle. Somewhere away from all these troublesome settlers, where a man could work in peace and make his pile. Tato's voice brought him back to reality. "What's that?" he muttered.

"It's easy, man," said Tato, clapping him on the back. "I'll arrange the gun. You get your friend Eduardo to pull the trigger, and there'll be fifty thousand reais in it for us. What do you say?"

Rayfran didn't hesitate. "Man enough to kill her?" He laughed. "Of course."

Tato heaved a sigh of relief. It wasn't such a big deal after all. Easily resolved. "I can get you a thirty-eight," he told Rayfran. "And tonight's the night, because she's sleeping over at Vicente's house, and not one of her young men is anywhere within reach. Pitch dark, raining heavily. Everyone will be asleep, and no one will hear a thing. All you guys have to do is steal over there later on, find a crack in the wall big enough for the barrel of a gun, and *poof*. One shot will do it. One shot and you get fifty thousand reais."

"What if the police get after us?" Rayfran was thinking more clearly now.

"Get after you?" Tato laughed. "How are they going to get after you? They won't even know who you are. No one will see anything, no one will hear anything, and by the time Vicente figures out what's happened, you'll have melted away into the woods. Oh, the police chief will make a show of investigating. But he won't find anything. His heart won't be in it. None of the authorities have any time for that woman—she's nothing but trouble."

Rayfran nodded. It sounded like a pretty good deal. Not that he personally had anything against her, but money was money. He'd have to find the opportunity to get Eduardo aside, and later on, after they'd had something to eat and maybe a shot of liquor, they'd head on over to Vicente's place.

After the chill of the night, Tato's *barraca* was friendly and familiar. Catarino and Cleoni were sitting astride their hammocks chatting, Curupira was stirring up a pan of beans, and Cabeludo was filing the chain for the saw. "Hey, boys," said Rayfran, stamping his feet and shaking the rain out of his hair, "is Eduardo here?"

"And if he is?" came a voice from a hammock strung in a corner.

"Well, if he is," said Rayfran, "you can tell him I have a deal for him."

"So what's your idea of a deal?"

Rayfran bent over the hammock and whispered in the ear of its occupant.

Across the road in Maria's house, they were finishing their meal and getting ready to turn in for the night. The hammocks had been tidily strung, the fire was glowing brightly in the clay stove, and the rain was pattering gently on the grass roof. The men were sitting on stools drinking coffee and talking about the planting season, and Nelda was helping Maria sort through the beans for the next day's lunch. She was feeling warm and comfortable and relieved that the day was safely over. There was much to look forward to. The meeting with the settlers, and then going back to Anapu and getting properly settled in. The last week had been a whirl of places and faces and traveling, and she was just about ready to get started on her new job.

Five hundred yards up the road in Vicente's house, everything was quiet. He and Dorothy had spent a long time talking, with the little girl curled up in her hammock listening to the soothing sound of voices. Before long she was sound asleep, and shortly after that Dorothy excused herself and took a candle out into the tiny cubbyhole where Vicente had rigged up a hosepipe for a makeshift shower. It was still raining, and the last thing she heard as she settled herself down on the thin mattress on the dirt floor was the sound of the raindrops falling on the roof. Sleepily she reviewed her conversation with Rayfran and Eduardo. The two men had appeared out of the woods after the conversation with Tato. She'd told them that they shouldn't be throwing grass around the settlers' fields. She'd explained the situation quite clearly. Why wouldn't they listen? Rayfran had bent over and told her in a low voice that whether she liked it or not, they were going to build that house. Over her dead body, if necessary. She remembered inviting them to the meeting and the look on their faces as they laughed. She remembered taking their hands and saying goodbye and God bless. And she asked God to soften their hearts and show them his goodness and love.

She was lying on her back snoring gently when they came for her. No one stirred as they crept out of the *barraca*; no dog barked as they walked up the road to Vicente's house. There was no sound, no light, nothing to indicate that anyone was there. The two men crept up to the house, held their breath, and listened. A very faint sound of snoring came from inside. But the walls were covered with black plastic, and although they walked around the house several times, they couldn't see a thing and they couldn't find anyplace where they could fit the barrel of the gun.

Nobody heard them when they crept back home. Rayfran removed his wet clothes, ducked under the ropes securing Catarino's hammock, and slipped into his own. He lay awake for a long time with his heart beating fast. Fifty thousand reais. Easy money. Tomorrow would be the day. He'd discussed it with Eduardo as they walked home from Vicente's house. Dorothy would be up early and would head straight for Manoel's *barraca* to get ready for the meeting. Past Vicente's house, up the steep little hill, there was a bend in the road where the trees grew high on either side—the perfect place for an ambush.

It was still dark when Nelda woke, and she couldn't see her watch to tell what time it was. Everyone was sleeping, and the only sound was from the rain on the roof. She turned over in her hammock, and pulling the thin sheet around her ears, she sank into a waking doze. Not time to get up yet. Then she heard two voices talking quietly and footsteps walking past. It's early to be up, she thought to herself as she closed her eyes and focused on her morning Hail Marys. Before she had got beyond the fifth repetition she had fallen asleep again.

Over in Vicente's house, Dorothy turned over, suddenly wide awake. It was dark and silent, but she could hear the gentle patter of the rain. She loved the rain. Always had. But it did make life difficult for people out in the backwoods. Everything took longer; the roads were slippery, the wood fires smoked, and everything smelled of mildew.

She yawned and stretched. She could feel her old bones creaking. The ole gray mare, she ain't what she used to be, ain't what she used to be . . . Dorothy smiled to herself. How she had loved to sing that as a child, never thinking that one day she'd be old and creaky and cranky. Just as well we can't see into the future, she thought as she turned over and settled back to sleep.

Tato opened his eyes and lay flat on his back, listening. He'd not heard a thing in the night. Why hadn't they woken him? He sat up and glanced around the room. All the hammocks were occupied. He swung his legs to the floor, felt around for his boots, turned them over and shook them out, and stuffed his feet into them. They were still damp and muddy from last night. Catarino didn't move, and Tato felt his way along the wall to Rayfran's hammock. He bent over the sleeping form. "Well?" he whispered.

Rayfran opened his eyes and dimly saw Tato's face. Tato leaned closer and put his lips to his ear. "Lost your nerve, did you?"

Rayfran sat up. "Couldn't see a frigging thing," he said. "But don't you worry, we'll finish the job today." He got out of his hammock, opened the door for a piss, and set to work getting the fire going for coffee.

Eduardo wandered over to the fire and groped around in the half-light for the dish of *farofa*. Manioc flour mixed with gristly chunks of meat, it filled the gap in his stomach while he was waiting for the first shot of coffee. Reaching into the waistband of his jeans, he missed the feel of the .38 and then remembered that he'd wrapped it in a cloth bag and hung it on a nail by his hammock. As he passed Rayfran, he whispered in his ear, "We're gonna make ourselves some easy money today."

Half an hour later the men were ready for work. Tato flirted with the idea of getting them all to go dig the truck out, but he had other things on his mind that morning. Coming up behind Rayfran, he hissed, "Don't screw up this time, OK?" and then walked off without looking back. The men straggled away in twos and threes, with Rayfran and Eduardo in the rear, carrying a barrel of grass seed. They were going to finish throwing the grass seed onto the clearing that had been made by Cícero. They'd almost completed the job, and the grass was sprouting already. In another few weeks there'd be no way that anyone could plant crops on that piece of land.

There was no sign of life in any of the houses as they walked off, and when they came to the bend in the road, they stopped. Eduardo put down the barrel of seed he had been carrying and sat on it while Rayfran checked their weapon. The chamber was full, but they'd need only one shot.

Dorothy was up and ready while Vicente was still taking his shower. "I'll go on ahead," she called out to him. "Let me make you some coffee," came the muffled response. "No need," said

Dorothy. "There'll be coffee at the meeting. And bread. I'll see you there."

Dorothy set off briskly up the road. As she passed the plastic shelter where Cícero lived, he poked his head out. "Good morning, Sister Dorothy," he said cheerfully. "How are you this morning? Bright and early, I see."

"That's right." She smiled at the tousled hair. "There's work to be done. Are you ready?"

"Not quite," he told her. "Just got to clean up a bit. But I wanted to ask if you could let me have a little rice. We've got none in the house."

"Sure I can," she told him. "There'll be plenty at the meeting, and I'll make sure there's some for you to take home, OK? We can't have you going hungry."

"Thanks, Sister," said Cícero. "You go on ahead and I'll catch you up."

Dorothy strode up the hill to where the road curved. As she rounded the bend, she saw Rayfran and Eduardo step out of the forest. For a moment she was startled. Were they coming to the meeting after all? "Good morning," she said, a little uncertainly. "Did you change your minds?"

"No, we're going to work," they said.

"Planting grass seed?"

They nodded.

"Oh, my dears," said Dorothy in her soft voice. "Don't do that. It's a crime to plant pasture on the settlers' fields."

"Let me ask you one thing," said Eduardo with a faint smile. "Do you like to eat beef?"

"Oh yes," replied Dorothy, smiling. "But there are plenty of cattle around, and this land belongs to the PDS, and they are going to plant cocoa. So I'm afraid you'll have to pull up that grass."

Eduardo sat down on the barrel and lit a cigarette. He didn't know why they were wasting time talking. Better to get the job over with before anyone came along. He winked at Rayfran, and then he heard that soft voice again.

"It's not your fault. I understand your position. You're only hired hands. But let me show you the map, and then you'll see for yourselves."

Dorothy opened her cloth bag, bent over, and spread the map on the red clay of the road. "We're here." She pointed to the road. "And this is the land that Tato is claiming. But INCRA says it belongs to the PDS."

Neither man was listening. Rayfran reached for the gun, but Eduardo shook his head almost imperceptibly and Rayfran held off. Dorothy stood up, folded her maps, and adjusted her glasses. "That's the situation," she told them. "And I'd best be off." She held out her hand, and Rayfran took it. Eduardo half rose, and she took his hand.

Dorothy turned to go, and Eduardo nodded. Rayfran pulled the gun. "Sister!" he shouted.

Dorothy turned back and saw the gun. She stood there for a minute, paralyzed. My God! she said to herself. He really means to kill me.

"Well, lady," she heard him say, "if we don't settle this business today, we'll never settle it."

Cícero splashed cold water over his face and hurried off after Dorothy. He couldn't imagine why she had gone up there alone.

Didn't she know it wasn't safe? That man Tato was a danger to everyone. Cícero had gone up to the site for the PDS headquarters only a few days earlier and seen Tato sitting on the wood that the settlers had cut. Well, he wasn't afraid of Tato, even after his house had been burned down, and he'd said straight out, "Look, Tato, this isn't your wood and it isn't your land either." And Tato had laughed in his face and said, "If you want to fight, we'll fight. And if I die, I'll take twenty settlers with me." Next day Tato had driven past in that gray truck of his and seen Cícero digging holes so that he could drive in some posts and build himself a tent. He'd backed up his car and shouted, "If you don't stop digging holes and get off my land, you know who's going to end up in those holes, don't you?"

Cícero rounded the corner and saw Eduardo seated on a barrel. Dorothy was standing close by, and Rayfran was pointing a gun at her. Cícero felt his heart lurch, and without stopping to think found himself in the forest, behind a big tree. Holding his breath, he looked around and saw Dorothy reach into her bag.

"Don't do this," she was saying to Rayfran. "Don't shoot me."

Rayfran tensed. "Take your hand out of your bag!" he shouted. "Is that a gun there or what?"

"I have no gun," she answered in her soft voice. "My only weapon is this." She pulled out her Bible and calmly opened it.

Rayfran and Eduardo watched her, mesmerized. Behind his tree, Cícero closed his eyes and said a quick prayer. Drawing on reserves she didn't know she had, Dorothy read in a level voice, "Blessed are the pure in heart, for they shall see God. Blessed are the meek, for they shall inherit the earth. Blessed are they who hunger and thirst after righteousness . . ."

She closed her Bible and looked into Rayfran's eyes. They were as hard as flint. "Well, lady," he spat at her, "that's enough of that."

The silence of the forest was shattered by a shot, and Dorothy fell to the ground. The last thing she saw was Rayfran's boots as he stood over her, emptying the chamber of his revolver. Everything went black.

The two gunmen turned without a word to one another and ran off into the forest. Cícero held his breath and watched them leave, and then, sobbing, he ran in the opposite direction as fast as his feet would carry him.

There was complete silence, and then, very gently, it started to rain on Dorothy's body as it lay in the road, mingling her blood with the red clay of the forest floor.

EPILOGUE

None of those involved in Dorothy's death could have had the smallest idea of the repercussions that would ensue, at local, national, and international levels.

On that rainy day in the forest, the settlers wept together and huddled inside, terrified that there would be more deaths. One or two of them crept stealthily through the forest to see for themselves whether or not she was really dead, but Dorothy's body was left in the rain until the police arrived at the end of the day. Someone set fire to Tato's car, and two of his workers were killed. Some say it was vengeance; some say they were silenced. Dorothy's body was taken to Belém, and a wake was held in the church of Santa Maria Goretti.

Numb with shock, Sister Julia was sitting in the church when she overheard one of the settlers talking to Dorothy. "It's all right, Sister Dorothy," he told her, "we're not burying you. We're planting a seed." The body was flown to Altamira and then to Anapu, where hundreds of mourners followed her coffin to the parish center at São Rafael and laid her to rest in the shade of a mango tree.

The government reacted with alacrity. Ministers were dispatched to the area and promised to bring peace and justice for the poor. Four days after the murder, an emergency meeting was held at the offices of INCRA in Belém. A joint mission consisting of INCRA, IBAMA, the federal police, the highway police, and the armed forces was sent to Anapu to carry out inspections and topographical surveys, regularize land claims, and maintain law and order. The minister of agrarian development announced a package of measures to be implemented within thirty days, including mapping, inspections, and disappropriation of idle land.

By June the indignant people of Anapu noted that little had been done. No roads had been improved, no surveys carried out, no land titles regularized. INCRA retorted that it had no resources: no computers, no maps, and no money. Furthermore, INCRA staff were unable to get into some of the disputed areas, which were heavily defended by hired gunmen. By September, Luis (whose *barraca* had been burned) announced that nothing had changed. Gunmen were everywhere, land invasions were continuing, and the rate of deforestation was increasing.

The police, however, acted with dispatch. On February 14 a warrant was issued for Tato's arrest, and two days later he turned himself in. Rayfran was arrested on February 20 and his accomplice, Eduardo, the following day. They confessed to the murder and told police that they had hidden out on Bida's *fazenda*, where they had buried the murder weapon. By March 8 the attorney general's office had indicted Rayfran and Eduardo for murder and Tato and Bida (who was in hiding) for being the masterminds of the crime. After some negotiation by his attorney, Bida turned himself in on March 27, and on April 8 Regivaldo was arrested. Of the five, he was the only one who resolutely maintained his innocence, even though he had been heard to say in January 2005 that there would be no peace in Anapu until Sister Dorothy had been dealt with. Cícero, the only witness to the murder, testified to the police and entered the recently established program of witness protection.

In April a request was made to the federal attorney general to federalize the crime, on the grounds that it was a grave violation of human rights, the state and federal judiciaries had been negligent in not protecting the victim, and the Republic of Brazil was a signatory to the International Convention on Human Rights. In June this request was reviewed by the Supreme Court and denied, because the action of the state judiciary had been both rapid and efficient and all suspects had been arrested and jailed.

Under increasing national and international pressure, and with assistance from the federal police, the two gunmen were brought to a jury trial on December 9, a record in the history of a state whose legal system was not known for being either efficient or impartial. The trial was attended by UN special *rapporteur* Hila Jalani, local dignitaries, Brazilian and international journalists, representatives of NGOs, family members, and sisters from the congregation of Notre Dame. Busloads of Dorothy's friends and supporters came from Anapu and set up a tent camp in the square outside the courthouse.

Neither Rayfran nor Eduardo contested his indictment. Rayfran was sentenced to twenty-seven years (which automatically granted him the right to a second jury trial), and Eduardo was sentenced to seventeen years with no retrial. Tato, Bida, and Regivaldo each contested his indictment, bringing actions for habeas corpus. Tato went on trial in April 2006, was convicted of being the intermediary, and was sentenced to twenty-seven years in prison, reduced to seventeen because of cooperation with the police. Bida's bid for habeas corpus was denied. On May 15, 2007, he was tried, convicted, and sentenced to thirty years' imprisonment. Regivaldo's bid for habeas corpus was accepted, and he is awaiting trial at liberty.

Despite considerable efforts by the public prosecutor's office and human rights groups both in the Amazon and farther afield, none of the other people mentioned in connection with

Dorothy's death—Luis Ungaratti, Délio Fernandes, Yoaquim Petrola, the mayors of Anapu and Porto de Moz, and members of the Barbalho family—was ever arrested. Which comes as no surprise to human rights activists in the area.

Dom Erwin, bishop of the Xingu, puts it this way: "The poor in the Amazon discover once again that for them there is no justice. He who has no money loses his cause, even if he is innocent. If he is poor, he will rot in jail. The rich will be freed to await trial at liberty, which means that they will never come to trial."

Among those who will never be accused in connection with

the murder, Dom Erwin speaks of those who clamored for Dot to be done away with, slandered her and accused her of arming the settlers, who went to the secret meeting in Altamira to plot her death, and who let off fireworks when they heard the deed was done. What sort of justice, thunders the bishop, is this?

And yet there is a kind of justice. Across the world, people hear the story of Sister Dorothy and are moved by it. Groups in Brazil, in the United States, and in Europe are keeping her memory alive by lobbying for land reform, for social justice, for simpler and fairer ways of living, for better care of our planet.

And in every tree seedling planted, every child enrolled in school, every family settled on the land, the legacy of Sister Dorothy lives on.

INDEX